PROFILES OF
WOMEN
PAST & PRESENT

PROFILES OF
WOMEN
PAST & PRESENT

Women's History Monologues for Group Presentations

VOLUME 3

Created, Researched and Written by Members of the
American Association of University Women
Thousand Oaks California Branch Inc.

Illustrated by Meryl O'Connor

AMERICAN
ASSOCIATION OF
UNIVERSITY
WOMEN

Thousand Oaks California Branch Inc.

ISBN 0-9637756-3-4

To order additional copies of this book, refer to the order form on page 96 or send a check for $14.95 per book (plus $2.50 shipping and handling for first copy, 50¢ for each additional copy; CA residents add sales tax) to:

AAUW/Profiles
Thousand Oaks CA Branch, Inc.
P.O. Box 4223
Thousand Oaks, CA 91359–1223

Include your name, address, phone number and organization and/or school district (if applicable) in all correspondence. For information on discounts for volume orders, write to the address above. We welcome questions and/or comments about your experiences with *Profiles of Women Past & Present*. Please send them to the address above.

The fifteen monologues in this book were researched, written, revised and edited by past and/or current members of the American Association of University Women, Thousand Oaks California Branch, Inc. We have made our best efforts to verify the accuracy of these histories, within the limitations of conflicting data and scarcity of original sources.

The notable women portrayed on the cover are (bottom row l to r): Ida B. Wells-Barnett by Shawna Andre; Dr. Eugenie Clark by Alice Wang; Mother Teresa by Nancy Guerrero; (top row l to r): Margaret Bourke-White by Kateri Alexander; Susan B. Anthony by Sandy Hindy; Fannie Farmer by Beverly Khoshnevisan; Ann Bancroft by Emily Schmidt; Dr. Ellen Ochoa by Marize Alphonso.

Cover Design: Michelle Webb
Cover Photo: Alan Raphael
Book Design: Deborah Davis
Editors: Kateri Alexander, Debbie Trice, Barbara Wilson

First Edition

Publisher's Cataloging-in-Publication Data
American Association of University Women, Thousand Oaks California Branch, Inc.
Profiles of women past & present: women's history monologues for group presentations, vol. 3; illustrations by Meryl O'Connor.
Includes bibliographical references.
ISBN 0-9637756-3-4
1. Monologues. 2. Women-Biography. 3. Drama in education.
I. American Association of University Women, Thousand Oaks California Branch, Inc.
II. Title. III. Series.
PN4305.M6 P77 2003 812.04508 LCCN 93-72554

10 9 8 7 6 5 4 3 2 1

Printed in the United States of America

This third volume of *Profiles of Women Past & Present* is dedicated to our own daughters, Stacey, Emily, Catherine, Julia Anne, Damien and Christine, and all young women creating their own profiles of women in the future.

Acknowledgements

We would like to acknowledge the many members, friends and supporters of the American Association of University Women, Thousand Oaks California Branch, Inc., who helped us shape a dream into a reality:

Lawrence C. Janss and the School of the Pacific Islands who granted the original funding for Volumes 1 and 2 of *Profiles of Women Past & Present*, and Kate McLean and the Ventura County Community Foundation who facilitated the funding of the grants;

The many members of the American Association of University Women, Thousand Oaks California Branch, Inc., who researched, wrote, edited and adapted the monologues, and presented them to schools and groups throughout our community;

The Women's History Publication Committee who compiled, designed, edited, produced and promoted Volume 3 of *Profiles of Women Past & Present:* Kateri Alexander, Colleen Briner-Schmidt, Deborah Davis, Sandy Hindy, Donna Langley, Betty Nordahl, Debbie Trice and Barbara Wilson;

The writers of the monologues: Kateri Alexander (Ann Bancroft), Joan Bennett (Margaret Bourke-White, Chien-Shiung Wu), Catherine Davis (Jerrie Cobb), Julia Anne Davis (Eugenie Clark), Ronda Eddleman (Susan B. Anthony), Cathy Ewbank (Mother Teresa), Beverly Khoshnevisan (Sor Juana Inés de la Cruz, Fannie Farmer, Harriet Tubman, Madam C. J. Walker), Joanne Knapp-Philo (Ida B. Wells-Barnett), Donna Langley (Agnes de Mille), Debbie Trice (Fannie Farmer), Barbara Wilson (Ellen Ochoa) and Kerri Yim (Dolores Huerta);

Additionally: Karl Alexander, Linda Barry, Amyra Braha, Darlene Daniel, Susan Girard, Kathy Heller, Pat Morgan, Sue Pelman, Liz Priedkalns and Deana Sun who assisted the publication committee;

And: Barnes and Noble Booksellers, Borders Books and Music, California Lutheran University, PAGES Books for Children and the Thousand Oaks Library;

The many people who reviewed the monologues and offered their expert advice to make them as accurate as possible: Mary M. Huth, University of Rochester, and Shannon M. Risk, The Susan B. Anthony House (Susan B. Anthony); Dr. Eugenie Clark; Ruth Lummis, Jerrie Cobb Foundation, Inc. (Jerrie Cobb); Ginger Carlson and Lynn Garafola, The Congress on Research in Dance (Agnes de Mille); Dr. Ellen Ochoa; Missionaries of Charity (Mother Teresa); A'Lelia Bundles (Madam C. J. Walker) and Nina Byers, Ph.D., UCLA (Chien-Shiung Wu);

And finally, our community for applauding our presentations and encouraging our endeavors.

Table of Contents

Prologue

What started as a mother's journey to show her daughter she could be anything she wanted to be when she grew up has evolved into a dynamic Women's History Project in our community and beyond. It also inspired us to publish three volumes of women's history monologues.

In 1985, seven-year-old Stacey Hindy broke her arm. While waiting at the doctor's office, she remarked that she might be a nurse when she grew up because "only men could be doctors." Her mother, Sandy, was shocked. How could her daughter believe her career possibilities were limited? After all, hadn't the Women's Movement opened all the doors?

After the doctor visit, Sandy researched and wrote four first person monologues similar to the ones in this book. Then, she presented them to the students at her daughter's school. One of the women she portrayed was Elizabeth Blackwell, America's first woman physician, demonstrating that girls could, indeed, be doctors when they grew up.

The next year, Sandy enlisted the help of the members of the Thousand Oaks California Branch of the American Association of University Women to research, write and present five women's history monologues in local schools during Women's History Month in March. Every year since then, the Thousand Oaks Branch of AAUW has organized an annual Women's History Project for our local schools. Some of our best monologues are included in this book. The dramatic portrayals allow audiences of all ages to be inspired by notable historic and contemporary women who overcame obstacles to achieve success in their lives and, in the process, helped shape our world.

In this volume, we introduce the lives of fifteen women who, with courage and determination, achieved the goals they set for themselves. Women like suffragist Susan B. Anthony, who was arrested, jailed and tried for voting—illegally—in the 1872 presidential election; Madam C. J. Walker, who became a self-made millionaire by producing and marketing her own brand of hair care products; Dolores Huerta, who left the teaching profession to become a political activist and co-founder of the United Farm Workers union.

We hope that the publication of *Profiles of Women Past & Present* will inspire women and girls to continue the journey one mother started. Today, her daughter, who once thought only men could be doctors, has completed her first year of medical school.

Introduction

This isn't a text book—it's a jumping-off point for your creativity. These short five-minute portrayals have been given in classrooms as part of our annual Women's History Project, but we have used them to enliven occasions throughout the year, including career days, science fairs, camp activities, meetings, Women's History Month celebrations—even nursing home visits. The possibilities are endless. Whether performed by a girl reading from note cards and wearing a homemade costume or by a professional actress, the excitement is the same: Women's History comes alive!

The monologues can be presented by women or girls. They can be simplified or adapted for particular audiences. With each monologue, we have included:

- A full-page illustration
- Suggestions for costume and props
- Notes/Tips for presenters
- Suggested resources
- A simplified version for pre-kindergarten through second grade audiences

If you organize a Women's History Project similar to ours in a school setting, you will probably need prior approval from the school district or principals in your area. You also may need to communicate with teachers, presenters and local news media. The Appendix includes samples of materials we have used for these purposes and other information you may find useful, including:

- Letters to school districts, school principals and classroom presenters
- Media release
- Public access television tips
- Announcement flyer
- Enrichment activities
- Suggested resources

The rewards for presenters are numerous. Months after the presentations, it's not unusual for students to meet presenters in our community and exclaim, "I know you! You're Eugenie Clark and you swam with the sharks!" or "Aren't you Ellen Ochoa? I'm going to be an astronaut when I grow up, too." It's gratifying to help children and adults realize there are no limits to the goals they set or the careers they choose at any age.

Suggestions for Presenters and Organizers

Being a presenter is a rewarding experience. For a short time, you are a famous historic or contemporary woman. To help you get started, we gathered the following suggestions from past presenters and organizers. We encourage you to use your creativity to make your portrayal a memorable experience for both you and your audience.

Recruiting Presenters

These monologues are suitable for presentation by adults or children. Acting experience and ability are not required. In our community, girls often portray these notable women at their schools.

Promoting Interest

When we organize our annual Women's History Project, we send out publicity to local newspapers, and radio and television stations. We also contact school and public libraries and ask them to display books about the women who will be portrayed, as well as other notable women, during Women's History Month in March. For several years, we have created Women's History Month bulletin boards at local libraries. We also have organized special events at book stores, libraries and other venues, creating promotional flyers to publicize such events.

Finding Costumes and Props

Costume shops can provide great ideas, but the best place to start looking for materials to create your costume and props is your own closet or your local thrift store. By asking friends, neighbors and relatives to help you find items you need, you'll be able to create a costume and gather necessary props at little or no cost.

Preparing for Your Performance

It's not necessary to memorize the monologue, but you should know it very well. Many presenters simply rehearse the monologues and read them aloud. Most presenters carry props that provide a place to hide a copy or outline of the monologue.

When girls are the presenters, it helps to have a teacher or adult volunteer coach them. The coach can set up a rehearsal schedule, help with costumes and props, set up the performance schedule and help make the experience a positive one for the girls.

Knowing Your Character

Each monologue is a very condensed version of one person's lifetime. If you are portraying a woman who is still alive, you should do some research to update the monologue and prepare yourself to answer questions your audience might ask.

Scheduling Your Time

If you are a classroom presenter, ask the teacher how much time you'll have to give your presentation and answer questions. You also might ask the teacher to introduce you and explain the purpose of your visit when you arrive. If time is limited, or if you don't feel comfortable answering questions, suggest that students go to the library or the Internet for more information.

Portraying Your Character

It's important to stay in character throughout your presentation to sustain the dramatic effect. When answering questions, respond in the first person, as if you are the woman you are portraying.

If you are portraying a woman of another race, it's helpful to let the audience know by using visual aids, such as drawings or photographs. Sometimes, our presenters wear a costume similar to what the woman in the monologue might wear. Then, holding a drawing or a photograph of the woman, they say, "I'd like to introduce you to a remarkable woman," and present the monologue in the third person.

Having Confidence

Have fun! Your audience will enjoy your portrayal. It won't occur to them that you may be nervous. Don't be afraid to be dramatic or to stand out. You are there to make an impression and you definitely will. Your audience will remember you for years to come. Enjoy yourself and the applause you will receive at the end of your portrayal.

SUSAN B. ANTHONY

Susan B. A...
"THE INVIN...
LECTU...
AT
Denver, Col...
Wednesday,

SUSAN B. ANTHONY (1820–1906)

Failure is impossible.

Imagine that you have a job—any job—like delivering newspapers or baby-sitting or walking dogs. Suppose that on payday your employer says, "Here is your money. But, because you're a girl, I'll only pay you half as much as I'd pay a boy." Would that be fair? Of course not! I spent my life fighting unfairness. I am Susan B. Anthony.

I was born in 1820 in Massachusetts, but I grew up in New York State. At that time, women couldn't keep the money they earned, go to college or vote. I was fortunate that my father belonged to the Religious Society of Friends, or Quakers. Quakers believe women and men are equals. They also believe in education for girls and boys, hard work and working to end injustice.

My father taught me to be independent. When I was 12, he hired me to work in his cloth mill. I worked 12 hours a day for two weeks and earned my first money. I used it to buy pretty teacups for my mother.

At age 19, I finished school and became a teacher. Teaching was the most respectable job a woman could have back then. But I was paid less than men who were teachers for doing exactly the same work. That made me angry. I believed I should receive "equal pay for equal services rendered." I protested, but it didn't make a difference. Other women would accept the unfair pay, so I had to accept it too—or quit.

After a few years, I *did* quit. Teaching didn't satisfy me. I wanted to work to end the injustice I saw in the world. I supported the temperance movement against the sale and use of liquor. People who drink too much cause a lot of problems. I was also an abolitionist. That means I worked to abolish, or end, slavery. Can you imagine? Americans owned other people and treated them like farm animals.

In 1851, I traveled to Seneca Falls, New York, for an abolition meeting. While I was there, I met Elizabeth Cady Stanton, a leader in the women's rights movement. We became lifelong friends and worked together for woman suffrage—the right of

Profiles of Women Past & Present

WOMAN SUFFRAGE LEADER

women to vote. We wrote long speeches supporting women's rights. I made many trips across the United States, giving the speeches and lecturing on women's rights.

When I spoke, I would say things like, "What we demand is that woman shall have the [vote], for she will never get her other rights until she demands them with the ballot in her hands." Often, the people in the audience would boo or call me names because they thought I was unladylike—and because they disagreed with me. But disapproval never stopped me. It challenged me to work harder.

In 1872, I voted in the presidential election. The 14th Amendment to the U.S. Constitution said all people born in the United States were citizens. It also guaranteed that no legal privileges, including the right to vote, could be denied to any citizen. I was a citizen, so wasn't I guaranteed the right to vote, too? I was arrested for voting illegally and tried in court. The judge decided I was guilty before my trial even started. He ordered me to pay a $100 fine, but I refused.

I started gathering signatures on a petition demanding that a woman suffrage amendment be added to the Constitution. Ten thousand people from 26 states signed. When I took the petitions to the U.S. Senate, the senators laughed. Every year after that, I appeared before Congress and tried, unsuccessfully, to get them to pass a woman suffrage amendment.

I made my last speech in 1906 when I was 86 years old. There were many young women in the audience that day and I told them, "The fight must not cease; you must see that it does not stop. Failure is impossible." Several weeks later, I died.

It took 14 more years for women to win the right to vote. In 1920, the 19th Amendment to the Constitution, also called the Susan B. Anthony Amendment, became law. It says, "The right of citizens of the United States to vote shall not be denied or abridged by the United States or any state on account of sex." I am proud that my work helped win the right to vote for all women who came after me.

COSTUME/PROPS

Black, mid-to-late 19th century style dress or skirt and blouse

Red shawl

Wire-rimmed glasses

Hair pulled back in a bun

Sign or flyers advocating women's right to vote

Leather satchel

NOTES/TIPS FOR PRESENTERS

According to Rheta Childe Dorr, Anthony possessed "a quality of leadership that amounted to genius." She quickly became "commander-in-chief" of the movement and remained so, even after she died. When Dorr interviewed Harriot Stanton Blatch (Elizabeth Cady Stanton's daughter) and other second-generation suffragists for her 1928 book, *Susan B. Anthony: The Woman Who Changed the Mind of a Nation,* they said they considered themselves Anthony's lieutenants.

Anthony had a strong chin, erect posture and a firm handshake. She often stamped her right foot for emphasis when speaking.

A red shawl became her trademark.

Anthony never married or had children because she did not want to give up her freedom and independence.

In 1979, Anthony became the first American woman honored on U.S. currency when the U.S. Mint issued a one-dollar coin with her likeness on its face.

SUGGESTED RESOURCES

DuBois, Ellen Carol, ed. *The Elizabeth Cady Stanton-Susan B. Anthony Reader: Correspondence, Writings, Speeches.* Rev. ed. Boston: Northeastern University Press, 1992. (Parts One through Three copyright 1981 by Schocken Books, Inc.)

Isaacs, Sally Senzell. *America in the Time of Susan B. Anthony: 1845 to 1928.* Crystal Lake, IL: Heinemann Library, 1999.

Kendall, Martha E. *Susan B. Anthony: Voice for Women's Voting Rights.* Berkeley Heights, NJ: Enslow Publishers, Inc., 1997.

Sherr, Lynn. *Failure is Impossible: Susan B. Anthony In Her Own Words.* New York: Times Books, 1995.

Weisberg, Barbara. *Susan B. Anthony.* Philadelphia: Chelsea House Publishers, 1988.

Not For Ourselves Alone: The Story of Elizabeth Cady Stanton and Susan B. Anthony. Dir. Ken Burns and Paul Barnes. VHS. PBS Home Video, 2002.

National Women's Hall of Fame. <http://www.greatwomen.org/>.

Not for Ourselves Alone. PBS. <http://www.pbs.org/stantonanthony/>.

The Susan B. Anthony House. <http://www.susanbanthonyhouse.org/>. (Select Biography.)

ANN BANCROFT

ANN BANCROFT (1955–)

I wanted to be 'the first'

to do something special.

Do you know where the North Pole is? You go north until you can't go north anymore—to the top of the world. I've been there. I've been to the South Pole and Antarctica, too. My name is Ann Bancroft and I'm a polar explorer.

When I was growing up, I knew, "I wanted to be 'the first' to do something special." But I couldn't imagine what it might be because school was really hard for me. I had a learning disability called dyslexia that made it hard for me to read or do math.

I was discouraged, too, because most of my friends knew what they wanted to do when they grew up, and I didn't. What I know now, though, is that everything you like and everything you do leads you to your grown-up life.

I grew up in Minnesota and I loved to be outside in all kinds of weather. Sometimes, I'd pull my sled across the snowy fields near my house and pretend I was far away exploring a place where no one had ever been before. I also canoed and backpacked and camped and climbed. Despite my learning difficulties, I went to college and became a physical education and special education teacher.

When I was 28 years old, I climbed Mt. McKinley in Alaska. It's 20,360 feet high. That's like climbing from your backyard to an airplane you can hardly see in the sky. It was very cold and dangerous, but I couldn't imagine staying home just because of the weather or the danger. After climbing Mt. McKinley, I wanted another adventure and I wanted it to be so important that it would be in *National Geographic* magazine.

I got my chance when I met a man who was leading a dogsled team to the North Pole. It sounded very exciting and I asked if I could go along. After he found out that I could ski and hike, he said, "Yes, but you'll be the only woman on the trip." We trained for the trip by living in the woods without heat or electricity or running water. I had to learn how to use a dogsled and how to care for the dogs. I also had to learn how to take photographs.

POLAR EXPLORER

On the trip, everyone wore warm polar suits, even when we slept. Sometimes, my face froze because it was 65 degrees below zero Fahrenheit. That's much colder than the freezer in your refrigerator. But I didn't let the cold stop me and, on May 1, 1986, I became the first woman to reach the North Pole by dogsled. It had taken 55 days to travel 1,000 miles. I had accomplished my goal of being "first" and my photographs would be in *National Geographic*.

I was so excited that, before I even got back home, all I could think about was making another trip—this time to the South Pole. I would go with a team of women only—no men and no dogs.

It took six years to raise enough money. In November, 1992, we started the 660-mile journey. We each pulled a sled piled high with 200 pounds of supplies. That's like pulling your parents up and down an icy route. It took us two months and one week, but on January 14, 1993, three of us became the "first all women's group" to ever ski to the South Pole while pulling sleds. We were the happiest women in the world. And I, of course, was ready for another adventure.

Eight years later, Liv (leev) Arnesen and I were the first women ever to ski 1,900 miles across the continent of Antarctica. The winds sometimes blew 90 miles an hour and the temperatures were usually 20 below zero. We skied from sea level to 11,000 feet. Sometimes, we attached sails to our heavy sleds, and skied and sailed across the frozen white ground. For 93 days, we had no chairs to sit on, we didn't see any other people and we couldn't take showers. But we didn't mind because we were doing what we loved most.

I've never loved anything more than stepping onto ice and snow that has never been stepped on before. So, the next time you fall on fresh snow to make a snow angel, close your eyes and think of yourself as an explorer like me. And then know that whatever your special dream is, someday you'll be telling your story of how you made it come true.

COSTUME/PROPS

Winter jacket or ski clothes

Winter scarf and mittens

Ski hat

Ski boots

Photograph of Bancroft with skis or sled

NOTES/TIPS FOR PRESENTERS

During the summer of 2002, Bancroft completed a 6-week adventure across the Great Lakes. Check her website for an update on this and future adventures.

Point out the North Pole, the South Pole and Antarctica on a map or globe.

Talk about the hardships involved in traveling such a long distance in frigid weather. What would you miss the most?

Ask students if they know what "snow angels" are. Explain that they are made by lying on your back in the snow, spreading your arms out from your body and moving them back and forth in the snow like wings. The impression left behind when you stand up is the snow angel.

Have students talk about some of the things they like to do best and what they might like to do when they grow up.

SUGGESTED RESOURCES

Loewen, Nancy and Ann Bancroft. *Four to the Pole!* North Haven, CT: Shoe String Press, 2001.

Ryan, Zoë Alderfer. *Ann and Liv Cross Antarctica: A Dream Come True!* Minneapolis, MN: yourexpedition, 2001.

Steger, Will. "North to the Pole: Five Men and a Woman Make Arctic History." *National Geographic*, September 1986, 289–317.

Wenzel, Dorothy. *Ann Bancroft: On Top of the World.* Minneapolis, MN: Dillon Press, 1990.

Poles Apart: The Journey of Ann Bancroft and the American Women's Expedition to the South Pole. Dir. Greg Stiever. VHS. Lead Dog Productions, 2000.

Bancroft Arnesen Explore. <http://www.yourexpedition.com/>.

National Women's Hall of Fame. <http://www.greatwomen.org/>.

Margaret Bourke-White

MARGARET BOURKE-WHITE (1904–1971)

Can you imagine not having television? How would you learn about the news? Well, you might read a newspaper, or listen to the radio, but it would be hard to *see* historic events unless they happened where you live. But if someone traveled around the world and photographed those events for magazines and books, you *would* see them. That's what I did. I traveled across the United States and around the world photographing historic events before there was television. I'm Margaret Bourke-White. I'm a photojournalist.

I was born in New York in 1904. When I was little, sometimes I pretended to take pictures, using an empty box as a camera. Then, when I was 8, my father took me to a factory to see machine parts being made. It was exciting! I wished I could capture what I was seeing with a real camera to show my friends.

You might think I studied photography when I started college, but I didn't. I went to five different colleges and changed my major many times. I studied engineering, biology and even herpetology—the study of reptiles and snakes—before deciding on photography. Then my mother surprised me with a camera. I had great fun learning to use it. When I needed to earn money to pay my tuition, I photographed the college campus and sold the pictures. When I graduated, I knew photography would be my career. "[The] world was full of discoveries waiting to be made.... [As a photographer] I could share the things I saw and learned."

One of my first projects was photographing men working in a steel mill. *Nobody* had done that before. Inside the dark steel mill, hot flames shot out of furnaces where the metal was melted. I crawled out onto high places to photograph the men pouring the liquid metal into molds to make steel machine parts. The heat burned my face, but it was worth it. Those pictures helped start my career.

I was hired to be a photographer by *Fortune* magazine. My first assignment took me to a meat-packing plant in Chicago. I photographed the meat-packing process there, start to finish. I made photo history with those pictures, because I didn't use words to tell the story. My photos told the story. It was the first-ever photo essay.

PHOTOJOURNALIST

In 1934, I traveled across farmland states turned into a "Dust Bowl" after years without rain. It was so dry, people wore masks over their faces to keep out the dust. I photographed scorched earth, dead animals and empty houses from the open cockpit of a two-seater airplane. My photos made people see how much others were suffering.

Another project took me to the southern United States. Many people there had no jobs and were very poor. In one town, I photographed two little girls who were twins. They took turns going to school, because they had only one coat and one pair of shoes between them. My pictures were in a book called *You Have Seen Their Faces*. When people read the book and saw my photos, they asked the government to help those poor people.

In 1936, I started working for a new magazine called *Life*. The editor sent me to Montana to photograph a large dam that was being built. My photograph of the Fort Peck dam was on the very first cover of *Life*, and my photo essay about the people building the dam was the lead—the most important story.

When World War II broke out in Europe, *Life* sent me there as a war correspondent. I was the first woman to photograph combat. I slept on the ground and washed myself with water scooped up in my helmet. I crawled through muddy fields with the soldiers and jumped into holes to dodge enemy fire. I was in danger, but while I was taking pictures, I was blind to everything around me—even danger. I was the first woman to fly on a bombing mission. Our plane was hit, but I got my pictures and we landed safely. Soon after, those pictures were in *Life* magazine under the headline "*Life's* Bourke-White Goes Bombing."

After the war, I photographed the Nazi death camps. My pictures of Holocaust survivors showed the world the horrible truth of what had happened.

My mother always told me to "open all the doors" and, for 25 years, I did just that. I got the stories no one else got, and I got them first.

COSTUME/PROPS

Khaki pants and shirt or World War II Air Force uniform

Tripod and camera bag

Old flash camera

Copies of Bourke-White's photos

NOTES/TIPS FOR PRESENTERS

Take flash photos of the audience when you come into the room.

Produce a class photo essay with photographs brought from home by students.

Bourke-White was a tireless perfectionist who often went without sleep and sometimes forgot to eat while taking photographs because her concentration was so intense. She was diagnosed with Parkinson's disease when she was 49.

SUGGESTED RESOURCES

Ayer, Eleanor H. *Margaret Bourke-White: Photographing the World.* New York: Dillon Press, 1992.

Bourke-White, Margaret. *Portrait of Myself.* Boston: G.K. Hall & Co., 1963. (Also excerpted by Jill Ker Conway, ed., in *Written By Herself: Autobiographies of American Women: An Anthology.* New York: Vintage Books, 1992.)

Horwitz, Margot F. *A Female Focus: Great American Photographers.* New York: Franklin Watts, 1996.

Rubin, Susan Goldman. *Margaret Bourke-White: Her Pictures Were Her Life.* New York: Harry N. Abrams, Inc., 1999. (Includes 56 of Bourke-White's photographs.)

Welch, Catherine A. *Margaret Bourke-White: Racing With a Dream.* Minneapolis, MN: Carolrhoda Books, 1998.

Gallery M. <http://www.gallerym.com/>. (Select Bourke-White from list of photographers.)

The Life Picture Collection. Life. <http://www.life.com/Life/gallery/movie.html>. (Select Bourke-White from list of photographers.)

National Women's Hall of Fame. <http://www.greatwomen.org/>.

EUGENIE CLARK

EUGENIE CLARK (1922–   )

I plan to keep diving and

researching… until I'm

90 years old.

Oh, hello! Please excuse my appearance. I just got back from a dive to study garden eels living on the sandy floor of the Red Sea. I'm Dr. Eugenie Clark.

I was born in New York City in 1922. My mother's family came from Japan and my father's from the United States. When I was a girl, my mother worked at a newsstand. On Saturdays, I went to work with her and she would let me go to a nearby aquarium. I spent hours staring at exotic fish swimming in the tanks. My favorite was the shark. I imagined what it would be like to swim with the sharks.

When I was 9, my mother bought me my first aquarium. Soon, I had many kinds of fish—everything from tiny guppies to colorful, tropical fish. I watched them carefully, drawing pictures and taking notes on their behavior. When I went to college, I decided to become an ichthyologist—a scientist who studies fish.

After I graduated, I was a research assistant at the Scripps Institution of Oceanography in California. While I was there, I learned how to collect and study fish, and how to dive deep into the ocean. My first dive was a disaster. There was a leak in the air line connected to my helmet. Suddenly, I couldn't breathe! Fortunately, I didn't get hurt, but it was scary.

Later, I traveled to the tropical Pacific islands of Micronesia to study poisonous fish. I went from island to island—diving, collecting fish specimens and making friends. The islanders taught me to use nets and spears to collect fish. Once, during a dive, a large shark swam right by me. At that moment, I remembered how I imagined swimming with the sharks when I was young. Now I had done it!

I wrote a book about my adventures in Micronesia called *Lady with a Spear*. Many people read it, including some wealthy people who wanted to start a marine laboratory. They asked me to be the founding director of the Cape Haze Marine Laboratory in Placida, Florida. Of course, I said yes.

The lab grew quickly and scientists from all over the country came to do research. I was one of the first scientists to study the

ICHTHYOLOGIST, SHARK EXPERT

learning behavior of sharks. I taught two sharks to bump their noses against a wooden target to ring a bell for food. My experiments taught me that sharks are intelligent. Now, the lab is located in Sarasota, Florida, and it's called Mote Marine Laboratory.

One day, a friend told me about an underwater cave in Mexico with "sleeping" sharks. I was puzzled. Like most people, I thought sharks had to swim all the time to keep breathing and didn't sleep. I decided to go to Mexico to see the "sleeping" sharks for myself. The first time I saw one, it really did look like it might be asleep. But when I swam very close, I saw the shark's eyes were open and its gills were moving. I took samples of the water in the cave and found there was enough oxygen for the sharks to breathe without swimming. So the sharks weren't sleeping—they were just resting in the underwater caves.

After my research in Mexico, I was ready for a new underwater adventure—this time in a small submarine called a submersible. Submersibles can go much deeper than divers can. While diving in submersibles, I've seen some incredible fish, including a shark the size of a motor home!

I'm not afraid of sharks, because most of the 370 shark species aren't dangerous to people. In fact, "you're much safer diving in shark-infested waters than you are driving your car to work." The only time I was injured by a shark, I *was* driving my car. I stopped suddenly and a shark jaw on the seat next to me fell against my arm. The teeth "bit" my arm and drew some blood!

Because I've studied sharks for so many years, people sometimes call me "Shark Lady." You might think now that I'm over 80, I'm getting too old to continue my work. But "I plan to keep diving and researching... until I'm 90 years old." I feel fortunate that I've been able to do what I love for so many years. I hope as you grow up, you'll find something you love to do and have the opportunity to do it your whole life.

COSTUME/PROPS

Outfit should resemble a diver's wet suit

Dive mask

Fins

Dive vest

Scuba diver's tank

Hair wet or gelled to look like you just came back from a dive

Photos of sharks or a shark jaw

NOTES/TIPS FOR PRESENTERS

Make a costume scuba tank using a large cardboard tube with an appropriately-sized ball glued to the top. Spray paint the tank blue, yellow or gray.

Display photos of sharks during the presentation.

Ask students if they are afraid of sharks; have ever been snorkeling or scuba diving; have an aquarium at home; have ever gone to an aquarium, Sea World, Mote Marine Laboratory, etc.

Let students practice taking careful notes and making detailed drawings of fish or sharks like Clark would do.

Although Clark is famous for her studies of sharks, she has also done substantial and important research on other marine species.

SUGGESTED RESOURCES

Butts, Ellen R. and Joyce R. Schwartz. *Eugenie Clark: Adventures of a Shark Scientist*. New Haven, CT: Shoe String Press, 2000.

Clark, Eugenie. "Into the Lairs of 'Sleeping' Sharks." *National Geographic*, April 1975, 570–584.

Clark, Eugenie. *Lady With a Spear*. New York: Harper, 1953.

McGovern, Ann and Eugenie Clark. *Desert Beneath the Sea*. New York: Scholastic, Inc., 1991.

McGovern, Ann. *Shark Lady: True Adventures of Eugenie Clark*. New York: Scholastic, Inc., 1978.

Ross, Michael Elsohn. *Fish Watching With Eugenie Clark*. Minneapolis, MN: Carolrhoda Books, 2000.

The Sharks. Dir. Jeff Myrow and Ed Spiegel. VHS. National Geographic, 1997.

Clark, Dr. Eugenie. *Home Page*. <http://www.sharklady.com/>.

Mote Marine Laboratory. <http://www.marinelab.sarasota.fl.us/>.

JERRIE COBB

JERRIE COBB
(1931–   )

Imagine you're flying high up in the air and you're in control. You know what every black switch and every red button is for, and you can steer not only left and right, but up and down, too. This is what I do. My name is Jerrie Cobb and I'm a pilot.

When I was 12, my father took me for a ride in his plane and I fell in love with flying. When I was 16, I got my pilot's license and flew "solo" for the first time. After that, I flew all over Oklahoma—my home state—doing odd jobs like washing and waxing airplanes, and giving people rides. I hung around country airports and learned about airplanes, inside and out.

By the time I was 18, I had the training to be a professional pilot. Because World War II had recently ended, there were plenty of trained pilots. Almost all of them were men. It didn't matter to me that, because I was a woman, it would be hard to find work as a pilot. I simply took the jobs that none of the men wanted.

One of my jobs was especially dangerous. I was hired by an airplane-shipping service to deliver planes to Peru. I crossed shark-filled oceans, thick green jungles and treacherous mountain peaks to reach my destination. One time, when I stopped in Ecuador, I was even arrested. They thought I was a spy!

I became one of the world's best pilots and set three international altitude, distance and speed records. My skills as a pilot attracted the attention of NASA—the National Aeronautics and Space Administration. The year was 1959 and NASA was doing top-secret tests on men to select the first astronauts for the American space program. Some people thought women should be tested, too, and I was asked to take the Mercury astronaut tests. They tested my ability to tolerate loneliness, pain and noise. They spun me, tilted me and dropped me into water.

I did better on the tests than most of the men and qualified to be America's first woman astronaut. In fact, I did so well that NASA decided to assemble a team of 13 women astronauts—the

PILOT, HUMANITARIAN

Mercury 13. I was so excited! It seemed to be only a matter of time before I would rocket into space.

My dream of flying in space didn't come true, though. NASA suddenly decided all astronauts must also be military test pilots. I understood what that meant. At that time, only men were allowed to be military test pilots, so NASA would not let the Mercury 13 women be astronauts. I tried to save the Mercury 13 program. I talked to NASA officials, members of Congress and even the vice-president of the United States. But they wouldn't change their minds and it was a long time before American women became astronauts. I was very disappointed, but I didn't give up my dream.

I decided to use my flying talents for a new purpose—to help the people living in the Amazon jungle of South America. The native people who live there are very poor. They live in small huts, and many are sick and hungry. It's hard to reach them by land because they live so far into the jungle, but I can get there by plane. The flights are dangerous and places to land are hard to find, but I'm dedicated to helping these people. I take them seeds and medicines and lots of love. I also fly them to hospitals when they're too sick for me to help them.

Except for my plane, I work alone. I return to the United States only once a year. The jungle is my home, and the native people are my friends and family. I eat, sleep, work and share my life with them. For my humanitarian work, I was nominated for the Nobel Peace Prize in 1981.

There's only one thing that would take me away from my work in the Amazon—the chance to go into space. "Nothing means more to me." Even though I'm over 70 years old, "I would do anything for the chance." I've heard people say "the sky's the limit," but to me it's a destination. Since I learned to fly so many years ago, my feet have hardly touched the ground. "I have this feeling that life is a spiritual adventure, and I want to make mine in the sky."

COSTUME/PROPS

Casual, contemporary aviator's clothing

Tailored summer shirt and slacks

Model plane

Supplies such as seeds and medicine bottles

Map of the Amazon River basin

NOTES/TIPS FOR PRESENTERS

Discuss the history and status of the U.S. space program in 1959.

After Cobb took the Mercury tests, NASA told her she would be the first woman in space. She never had that opportunity. Instead, in 1963, the Russians sent Valentina Tereshkova into space. Cobb had just finished testifying before the House Space and Astronautics Committee to gain support for the Mercury 13 women. John Glenn, other astronauts and officials testified against the women. Twenty years later, in 1983, Sally Ride was the first American woman to go into space.

Although Cobb spends most of her time in South America, she keeps up to date with the U.S. space program. Her supporters have launched a campaign to put her on a Space Shuttle mission.

The 1981 Nobel Peace Prize was given to the Office of the United Nations High Commissioner for Refugees.

SUGGESTED RESOURCES

Cobb, Jerrie. *Woman Into Space: The Jerrie Cobb Story.* Englewood Cliffs, NJ: Prentice-Hall, 1963.

Cobb, Jerrie. *Solo Pilot.* Sun City Center, FL: Jerrie Cobb Foundation, Inc., 1997.

Freni, Pamela S. *Space for Women: A History of Women With the Right Stuff.* Santa Ana, CA: Seven Locks Press, 2002.

Haynsworth, Leslie and David Toomey. *Amelia Earhart's Daughters: The Wild and Glorious Story of American Women Aviators from World War II to the Dawn of the Space Age.* New York: William Morrow and Company, Inc., 1998.

Female Frontiers. NASA. <http://quest.arc.nasa.gov/space/frontiers/cobb.html>.

Mercury 13: The Women of the Mercury Era. <http://www.mercury13.com/>.

AGNES DE MILLE

AGNES DE MILLE (1905–1993)

It was 1943—the middle of World War II. No one dreamed a Broadway musical about farmers and ranchers in Oklahoma would be a big hit. Richard Rodgers composed the music. Oscar Hammerstein wrote the words. And Agnes de Mille—that's me—I created the dances. I'm a choreographer.

Broadway musicals always included dances, but in *Oklahoma!* my dances helped tell the story. This was a first. I didn't choose my dancers because they were pretty, as directors often did. I chose them because they could act and dance.

I always loved to dance. When I was very young, I'd whirl around for anyone who cared to watch. In 1914, when I was 9, my family moved from New York to California. My uncle, Cecil B. DeMille, was making movies and asked my father, who wrote plays, to join him. My sister, Margaret, and I found it exciting to be excused from school to watch movies being filmed. I dreamed of becoming an actress until Mother took me to see the great ballerina, Anna Pavlova. From then on, I wanted to be a dancer. I begged to take dance lessons, but my father thought "nice girls" did not become dancers.

I was lucky when my sister developed a foot problem, because her doctor thought dance lessons might help. We both enrolled at Theodore Kosloff's School of Imperial Russian Ballet. My teacher thought I was too old to start dancing. I was 14. If you want to be a ballet dancer, you must begin when your body is growing. Also, I didn't have the ideal shape for a ballerina—long arms and legs and a small, compact body. But I had real acting ability, I was creative and, boy, could I jump! I studied and practiced dance all through high school and college, too.

Right after I graduated from college, my parents divorced, and my mother, sister and I moved back to New York. I studied dance and created my own dances. Nobody would pay to see me dance, so my mother sponsored dance concerts for me and gave tickets to her friends to fill the seats. I got good reviews, but I couldn't find a steady

DANCER, CHOREOGRAPHER

job as a dancer. So I went to England where I studied dance and choreography, and created my first real group dances. Six years later, I returned to New York. I felt my youth was gone. I had no money, no husband, no child, no achievement in work.

Then, in 1942, a friend told me that a Russian ballet company was looking for a new ballet with an American theme. I presented my idea of a feisty cowgirl out to win the heart of a young cowboy and they liked it. Aaron Copland, the great American composer, wrote the music. The ballet was called *Rodeo* (roh-DAY-oh).

I always told stories with my dances and gave my characters real feelings. I often used movements from folk dances, such as square dancing. For *Rodeo*, I created horseback riding and roping movements. I also used tap dancing for the first time in a ballet. It was quite a challenge teaching Russian ballet dancers to act like cowboys.

On opening night, I danced the role of the feisty cowgirl. If it is possible for a life to change at one given moment—that was my moment. Chewing gum and squinting under a Texas hat, I did what I had been preparing for my whole life—I danced. The audience called us back 22 times to take bows. Later, my father came to a performance. After the show, he had tears in his eyes when he told me how proud he was.

Suddenly, everything was right in my life. Rodgers and Hammerstein asked me to choreograph *Oklahoma!* and I fell in love with a man I met through the famous choreographer, Martha Graham. We got married and had a son. I choreographed other shows, such as *Brigadoon* and *Carousel*, which I also directed. I wrote books about my life and about dance.

When I was 70, I suffered a stroke that paralyzed my right side. Slowly, I learned to write with my left hand and to walk using a cane. I continued my work for several years after that. On my tombstone I wanted only one word: "Dancer." For, "to dance means: to step out on the great stages of the world, to flash and soar... to ride violins and trumpets... to feel the magic work."

COSTUME/PROPS

Ballet slippers

Leotard

Or, full-skirted gingham dress

Or, western denim pants, shirt, boots and hat

Hair in ponytail

Posters for musicals de Mille choreographed

NOTES/TIPS FOR PRESENTERS

Play some of the music from *Oklahoma!* or *Rodeo* before you begin to speak.

Demonstrate or teach a dance step or two during or after your presentation.

Show a scene from the movie *Oklahoma!* Agnes de Mille choreographed the movie version, as well as the play.

Ask students if they have ever seen the musicals mentioned in the monologue.

Musicals choreographed by Agnes de Mille include: *Oklahoma!* (1943), *Bloomer Girl* (1944), *Carousel* (1945), *Brigadoon* (1947), *Gentlemen Prefer Blondes* (1949), *Paint Your Wagon* (1951), *The Girl in the Pink Tights* (1954), *Kwamina* (1962) and *110 in the Shade* (1963).

SUGGESTED RESOURCES

de Mille, Agnes. *To A Young Dancer.* Boston: Little, Brown and Co., 1962.

de Mille, Agnes. *Where the Wings Grow.* New York: Doubleday and Co., Inc., 1978.

Easton, Carol. *No Intermissions: The Life of Agnes de Mille.* Boston: Little, Brown, 1996.

Gherman, Beverly. *Agnes de Mille: Dancing Off the Earth.* New York: Athenaeum, 1990.

The Kennedy Center Honors: Agnes de Mille. The John F. Kennedy Center for the Performing Arts. <http://www.kennedy-center.org/programs/specialevents/honors/history/honoree/demille.html>.

Fannie Farmer

FANNIE FARMER
(1857–1915)

Can you cook? Well, if you'd like to learn, just ask me. My name is Fannie Farmer and I'm a cooking teacher.

One hundred years ago, I was the most famous cooking teacher in the United States. I was so famous a candy company paid me to let them put my name on their candy. I didn't have anything more to do with making their candy than Michael Jordan does with making basketball shoes. But the companies knew, if they used our names, more people would buy their products. And they were right! Fanny Farmer candy is still sold today.

I'll bet you're wondering why I was so famous. After all, being a cooking teacher probably doesn't seem as important as being a basketball star.

When I was young, cooking was hard work. We didn't have frozen food or microwaves. Stoves were a new invention, but they didn't have buttons or dials to turn them on and set the temperature. Instead, you built a fire inside the stove, and opened or closed air vents to make it hotter or cooler. Believe me, it wasn't easy.

I was born in Boston, Massachusetts, in 1857, the oldest of four sisters. I wanted to be a teacher when I grew up but, before I finished high school, I got very sick and couldn't move my legs. It took me several years to get well. As you can see, I still walk with a limp.

With no high school diploma, I thought I'd have to give up my dream of teaching. But my sister encouraged me to go to the Boston Cooking School to learn to be a cooking teacher. It's funny, I wasn't even the best cook in my family. I often burned the cookies I baked.

I was 32 years old when I graduated from the Boston Cooking School. I couldn't find a job, so I taught my friends' daughters how to cook. One day I taught them how to measure flour. *(Hold up spoon and demonstrate.)* For a rounded tablespoon, you fill the spoon to overflowing, then shake it gently until there's the same amount of flour rounded up above the spoon as there is in the spoon. One girl complained, "If I do it that way, I might get it different every time. Why not use two level spoonfuls?"

Cooking Teacher, Author

She was right. From then on, I taught my students to use *only* level measurements. After all, "correct measurements are absolutely necessary to insure the best results."

Soon after that, the Boston Cooking School hired me to teach there. Before long, I became the principal. When I rewrote a cookbook written by an earlier principal, I replaced all the rounded measurements with level ones. I also had the students test the recipes to make sure they tasted good and that the instructions were correct. I advertised my cookbook as the first to be kitchen-tested.

That book—*The Boston Cooking-School Cook Book*—was first published over a hundred years ago in 1896. Since then, other cooks have updated it, and it's still a best seller under the name, *The Fannie Farmer Cookbook*. Many young women and men have used my book to learn to cook, because it clearly explains everything they need to know.

I wanted to teach people how to cook for their families, but the Boston Cooking School only trained students to teach cooking in public schools or to run cafeterias. So, I left the Boston Cooking School and started my own school—Miss Farmer's School of Cookery. I wanted my students to enjoy preparing food at home. I had "no patience with cooks who just boil their vegetables, instead of putting heart and soul into cooking so that it becomes enjoyable instead of drudgery."

I wrote many cookbooks, but the one I'm proudest of is *Food and Cookery for the Sick and Convalescent*. What do you want to eat when you're sick? Something that tastes good, or something that is good for you? Of course, you want food that looks good—and tastes good, too. My book had recipes for good-tasting food that would help sick people get better.

I never stopped teaching, even when I became ill again and had to use a wheelchair. I taught my last class two weeks before I died in 1915. In my day, I was called "the Mother of Level Measurement," but today, I'm best known as the author of *The Fannie Farmer Cookbook*.

COSTUME/PROPS

Apron

Long skirt or dress

Hair piled on top of head

Pince-nez (small eyeglasses that clip on the nose)

Measuring spoons

Mixing bowl with flour

The Fannie Farmer Cookbook and/or *The Boston Cooking-School Cook Book*

Fanny Farmer candy

NOTES/TIPS FOR PRESENTERS

Walk with slight limp. This monologue can be adjusted for performance from a wheelchair.

Replace Michael Jordan and basketball shoes with a current star and licensed product.

Discuss product licensing. Note that Farmer's first name is spelled "Fanny" on the candy. This is not an accidental misspelling. Farmer required it as part of the licensing agreement.

Ask how many have used a cookbook to make something.

Serve some food at your presentation. Show how much more fun food is when it is garnished. Try sprinkles, powdered sugar, etc.

Much of the published information about Fannie Farmer is inaccurate. *Perfection Salad* (cited below) and scholarly reference works are the best sources.

SUGGESTED RESOURCES

Cunningham, Marion. *The Fannie Farmer Cookbook.* New York: Knopf, 1996.

Farmer, Fannie Merritt. *Original 1896 Boston Cooking-School Cook Book.* Facsimile edition. Mineola, NY: Dover Publications, 1997.

Scobey, Joan. *The Fannie Farmer Junior Cookbook.* London: Little, Brown & Co., 2000.

Shapiro, Laura. *Perfection Salad: Women and Cooking at the Turn of the Century.* New York: Farrar, Straus & Giroux, 1986.

About Fannie Farmer. About, Inc. <http://womenshistory.about.com>. (Search for Fannie Farmer in this topic.)

DOLORES HUERTA

DOLORES HUERTA
(1930–   )

"It's not enough to care about what's wrong, you've got to do something to make it better." I thought about that often when my students came to school hungry or needing shoes. Their parents were farm workers in the fields. Their work was hard, their days were long and their pay was little. I thought I could do more to help my students if I helped their parents work together to get better pay and working conditions. A person who convinces people to work together for change is called a political activist. That's what I do. My name is Dolores Huerta (HWAIR-tah).

I was born in 1930 in the state of New Mexico. My father was a miner, a migrant worker and a political activist. My parents divorced when I was very young and my mother raised my sisters, brothers and me by herself. It was hard being a single parent and working all the time, but my mother was a constant source of support to me. She taught me an important lesson in life—perseverance. Perseverance means you keep trying, even when you don't succeed the first time. My grandfather called me "seven tongues" because I talked a lot. That has been a good thing. You need to be able to talk to people to help them.

When I was a girl, I took dance lessons and dreamed of being a dancer. But in college, I decided to be a teacher, instead, because I wanted to help people. I was hired to teach the children of farm workers in central California, but I didn't teach very long. "I thought I could do more by organizing farm workers than by trying to teach their hungry children."

After I left teaching, I worked for the Community Services Organization. One of my jobs was registering Mexican-Americans to vote in elections. Voting is a right held by every American citizen. When you vote, you have a say in how your government is run.

While I was working with the Community Services Organization, I met a man named César Chávez. Together, we held meetings in the homes of farm workers and talked about what could be done to make their lives better. In 1962, we officially organized the

POLITICAL ACTIVIST, UNION ORGANIZER

United Farm Workers labor union. A labor union is a group of workers who join together to help each other get better pay and working conditions. At first, farm owners didn't believe their workers could work together as a group. Then, they refused to recognize that the union represented, or spoke for, all of the workers.

I did many things to help the union. I organized big meetings called rallies where workers could share ideas. The union asked for—and eventually won—many basic rights, because when everyone stands together and demands change, many people listen. Can you imagine working all day and not being able to go to the bathroom, or not having fresh water to drink, or not earning enough money to buy food and pay your rent? That's what life was like for most farm workers before the United Farm Workers union.

In 1965, I helped organize a strike against California grape growers who would not recognize the union. A strike is when all the workers agree to stop working in order to get what they want. It takes a lot of courage to strike, because you may not win and sometimes you even lose your job. The union farm workers stopped picking grapes. Then, people all over the United States stopped buying—or boycotted—grapes to show support for the farm workers. The growers stopped making money because people weren't buying their grapes. Finally, five years later, the growers agreed to work with the United Farm Workers. When the strike ended, I helped the union and the growers figure out how to work together.

Today, I spend much of my time traveling across the country promoting "La Causa" (lah COW-sah)—the farm workers' cause—and also women's rights. I'm proud to be the mother of eleven children who have grown up to be political activists like me. I expect all my children, grandchildren and great-grandchildren to have faith in themselves and to work together to build a better world. I expect all of you to do that, too. Do I believe it's possible to build a better world? "¡Sí, se puede!" (see say PWEH-they)—Yes, it can be done!

COSTUME/PROPS

Jeans and T-shirt or business attire

Political button

Megaphone, or microphone and loud speakers for rallies

Picket sign

NOTES/TIPS FOR PRESENTERS

Discuss the power of the consumer. Explain what a boycott is and how it works.

Ask students what they can do to make the world a better place to live in today and when they grow up.

"¡Sí, se puede!" (Yes, it can be done!) is the United Farm Workers motto. When Huerta is a speaker at a meeting or rally, she will extend her fist in the air and lead the audience in shouting this motto to motivate them.

Huerta is a small woman, only 5 ft. 1 in. tall. She is known for her great stamina. In her *Ms.* magazine article cited below, Julie Felner states that Huerta views every moment as an organizing opportunity, every person as a potential activist and every minute as a chance to change the world.

SUGGESTED RESOURCES

DeRuiz, Dana C. and Richard Larios. *La Causa: The Migrant Farmworkers' Story.* Austin, TX: Steck-Vaughn, 1993.

Felner, Julie. "For a Lifetime of Labor Championing the Rights of Farmworkers." *Ms.*, January/February 1998, 46–9.

Ferriss, Susan and Ricardo Sandival. *The Fight in the Fields: César Chávez and the Farmworkers Movement.* New York: Harcourt Brace, 1997.

Lindop, Laurie. *Champions of Equality.* New York: Twenty-First Century Books, 1997.

Perez, Frank. *Dolores Huerta.* New York: Steck Vaughn, 1996.

Dolores Huerta Biography. United Farm Workers of America. <http://www.ufw.org>.
(Select History, then Dolores Huerta Biography.)

National Women's Hall of Fame. <http://www.greatwomen.org/>.

SOR JUANA INÉS DE LA CRUZ

Sor Juana Inés de la Cruz (1648 or 1651–1695)

God has given me the gift of a very profound love of truth.

As a child who "burned with the desire to know," I never imagined that I would one day defend the right of women to think and learn. But when I grew up, I did that in my writing. I am Sor Juana Inés de la Cruz—Sister Juana Inés of the Cross.

I was born over 350 years ago in New Spain—or Mexico, as it is called today. The name given to me at birth was Juana de Asbaje y Ramírez. My father didn't live with us, so my mother, sisters and I lived with my grandfather. In those days, it was thought that women couldn't live on their own. We didn't have much money, but if you value knowledge, as I did, we were very rich indeed. My grandfather had many, many books.

When I was just 3 years old, I followed my sister to school so I could learn to read. Later, I heard about a school in Mexico City where science was taught. But girls were not allowed to attend. I begged my mother to dress me as a boy and send me to that school, but she said no. So I learned Latin, mathematics, science, history and literature from the books in my grandfather's library.

When my grandfather died, I was sent to Mexico City to live with an aunt and uncle. They were wealthy and lived in a fine house where I had many opportunities to learn. My uncle was a friend of the viceroy, an important man sent by Spain to rule in Mexico. When I turned 13, the viceroy's wife invited me to live at the palace and be her lady-in-waiting. Life there was exciting! I attended plays, concerts and dances. I often wrote poems and plays celebrating social or political events. My intelligence impressed the viceroy and, when I was 15, he invited 40 university professors to the palace to ask questions to test my knowledge. No one asked a question I couldn't answer.

When the viceroy returned to Spain, I had to find another place to live. I couldn't marry, because I had no dowry—money to give to a husband. So I decided to enter a convent and be a nun. A friend told me of a special convent where I could continue to write

POET, SCHOLAR

and study. I found patrons—wealthy people to pay my convent fees—and I wrote poems for them. When I entered the convent, I took the name Sor Juana Inés de la Cruz. I lived comfortably in a cell—an apartment—within the convent. It had several rooms, including a library. I had a large collection of books, as well as musical and scientific instruments. I even had a servant to help me.

I wasn't allowed to leave the convent, but people could come and visit. I often entertained friends and scholars with music, discussions and lively debates. I wrote and sold plays, poetry, songs and essays to pay my expenses. In my writing, I spoke for slaves, Indians, women and others who were mistreated by the church or the government. I published three volumes of poetry and became famous.

As my fame grew, many people were jealous or afraid of my work. Then, I was tricked into writing a letter which put me in the middle of a disagreement between two church leaders. The bishop in charge of my convent told me to stop writing about worldly subjects and to write, instead, only about religious matters. I wrote him a long letter defending my right to pursue my life as a writer and scholar. I wrote, "God has given me the gift of a very profound love of truth. Since I was first struck by the lightning flash of reason, my propensity for learning is so strong… that neither outside censure nor my own second thoughts… have been able to stop me from pursuing this natural impulse."

The bishop disagreed with my reasoning and pressured me to stop writing. I couldn't convince him to change his mind, so I gave up my writing and renounced my love of books and learning. I sold the 4,000 books in my library, gave the money to charity and retreated to a quiet life in the convent.

I died a year later, in 1695, while caring for my sisters in the convent when a terrible plague struck Mexico City. Even today, I am remembered as one of the greatest women poets of Mexico.

COSTUME/PROPS

White nun's habit and wimple with black veil

Large cross on heavy chain

Writing paper and quill pen

Books

NOTES/TIPS FOR PRESENTERS

The pronunciation for Sor Juana Inés de la Cruz is: sore HWAH-nah ee-NESS deh lah CREWTH. Juana de Asbaje y Ramírez is: HWAH-nah day ahs-BAH-hay ee rah-ME-reth.

References differ on the birth date of Sor Juana Inés de la Cruz. It was originally thought to be in 1651, but new research suggests it may have been 1648.

No one is certain why Sor Juana Inés de la Cruz gave up writing and renounced her love of books and learning. Some sources suggest it was voluntary and others imply it was forced. One source stated she took the mystery of her renunciation to her grave.

SUGGESTED RESOURCES

Juana Inés de la Cruz, Sor. Amanda Powell, translator. *The Answer/La Respuesta.* New York: Feminist Press, 1994.

Martinez, Elizabeth Coonrod. *Sor Juana: A Trailblazing Thinker.* Brookfield, CT: Millbrook Press, 1994.

Marting, Diane E., ed. *Spanish American Women Writers.* New York: Greenwood Press, 1990.

Thompson, Kathleen. *Sor Juana Inés de la Cruz.* Milwaukee: Raintree Publishers, 1990. (This book tells her story in English and Spanish.)

"Sor Juana Inés de la Cruz." *Sunshine for Women.* February 1999. <http://www.pinn.net/~sunshine/march99/cruz2.html>.

Sor Juana Inés de la Cruz. University of Arizona Women's Studies class. <http://info-center.ccit.arizona.edu/~ws/ws200/fall97/grp10/grp10.htm>.

ELLEN OCHOA

ELLEN OCHOA
(1958–   )

Have you ever watched a Space Shuttle launch on TV and wished you were an astronaut blasting off into space? When I was your age, the only Americans who traveled in space were military test pilots, and all of them were men. But when Sally Ride became the first American woman in space in 1983, I realized I could be an astronaut, too. I'm Dr. Ellen Ochoa (oh-CHO-ah). I was the first Mexican-American woman to travel in space.

I was born in Los Angeles in 1958. My parents divorced when I was in junior high school and, after that, my mother raised my sister, three brothers and me by herself. She showed us that, with an education, we could be anything we wanted to be. She took college classes for 22 years, earned a college degree and worked for a newspaper.

I always worked hard to do my best in school. My favorite subjects were math, English and music. I played the flute and thought about being a musician. When I graduated from high school, I had the highest grades in my class.

When I started college, I changed my mind several times before deciding on a career in math or science. My favorite classes were math and physics. Physics is the science of matter and energy—learning about things like motion, light and sound. I was also interested in engineering—using science and math to design and build things. I talked to an engineering teacher about taking classes and he said engineering was too hard for women. So, I took more physics classes and earned a degree in physics. I wanted to do research, so I went to Stanford University and earned both a masters and a doctorate degree in electrical engineering. That teacher who told me engineering was too hard for women was definitely wrong!

Some of my friends at Stanford applied to NASA—the National Aeronautics and Space Administration—to become astronauts. The space program was growing, and it needed more scientists and engineers as astronauts. I was qualified, so I applied.

While waiting for NASA to decide, I worked as a researcher on optical recognition. Using lasers and holograms, my team and I invented and patented three optical systems which help computers "see."

ENGINEER, INVENTOR, ASTRONAUT

Later, I supervised 35 scientists and engineers working on optical systems for NASA. I also took flying lessons and got my pilot's license.

In 1990, NASA selected me for the astronaut training program. That year, I also got married and moved to Houston for my training. Astronaut training was challenging. We studied geology, meteorology, astronomy and many other subjects. We experienced weightlessness by flying in a jet plane. When we got up in the air, the pilot flew the plane up and down like a roller coaster and, as we went down, we were weightless. We learned about the Space Shuttle—inside and out—and used a Shuttle simulator to practice handling problems we might encounter in space.

So far, I've been to space four times. My first mission was in 1993 aboard the Space Shuttle Discovery. I was a mission specialist. Mission specialists are in charge of science experiments. I operated the Remote Manipulator System, or robotic arm, to launch and retrieve a satellite. The robotic arm is a 50-foot long mechanical arm with wrist, elbow and shoulder joints just like your arm has. To operate it, I used hand controllers—similar to the hand controllers you use for video games. I used the robotic arm again during my second mission to retrieve another satellite.

My last two missions were to the ISS—the International Space Station. The ISS is a laboratory in space where scientists from around the world live and work together. In 1999, we completed the first-ever docking with the ISS to deliver clothing, computers, tools and other equipment. In 2002, we delivered the first of nine trusses—supporting beams—to expand the ISS. During the missions, "the most exciting thing was looking out at Earth from up there. It was beautiful."

I hope you're excited about science, and maybe even thinking about being a scientist or an astronaut when you grow up. I've had many opportunities to stand out because I worked hard and got a good education. Education will give you opportunities to stand out, too. "A good education can take you anywhere on Earth and beyond."

COSTUME/PROPS

Blue jumpsuit or blue shirt and slacks with NASA patch and name badge

Space Shuttle model or photo

Photo of robotic arm

NOTES/TIPS FOR PRESENTERS

Update this presentation with Ochoa's additional space flights after STS-110 in 2002.

Ochoa enjoys talking to students about her experiences in space and how important she believes education is. She is proud of her Mexican-American heritage and strives to be a role model for all students so they will be encouraged to work hard in school and become whatever they want to be.

The NASA website is an excellent source of information about the space program.

SUGGESTED RESOURCES

Oleksy, Walter. *Hispanic-American Scientists*. New York: Facts on File, Inc., 1998.

Romero, Maritza. *Ellen Ochoa: The First Hispanic Woman Astronaut*. New York: PowerKids Press, 1997.

St. John, Jetty. *Hispanic Scientists*. Mankato, MN: Capstone Press, 1996.

Biographical Data: Ellen Ochoa. NASA: Lyndon B. Johnson Space Center. <http://www.jsc.nasa.gov/Bios/htmlbios/ochoa.html>.

Human Spaceflight. NASA. <http://spaceflight.nasa.gov/>.

MOTHER TERESA

MOTHER TERESA
(1910–1997)

Peace begins

with a smile.

When something bad happens to a homeless person, some people think, "Who cares? That's just a bum." I believe God cares. And I believe God wants me to care. I was born Agnes Gonxha Bojaxhiu, but you probably know me as Mother Teresa.

My life began in Albania in 1910. My family always called me Gonxha (GOHN-jah)—my middle name, which means "flower bud"—because I was plump and rosy. I was a happy girl who loved to run and play games with my sister and brother. We were devout Catholics and I often went with my mother to take food or money to the needy.

When I was 9, my father died. We lost everything but our home. My mother started a small business. She even sent my sister and me through high school, which was quite an accomplishment for girls at that time.

During those years, Catholic missionaries would tell our villagers about their work with poor people in India. This made a great impression on me. By the time I was 18, I knew that, above all else, I wanted to become a nun and help the poor. I left my home to join the Sisters of Loreto and never saw my mother or sister again.

As a nun, I promised three things: to remain without possessions, to be pure in mind and body, and to obey my religious superiors. I chose a new name—Teresa—for St. Therese, sometimes called "the Little Flower," who believed that good comes from doing simple things well and with extraordinary love. I was sent to Ireland to learn English, and then to India, where I learned Bengali.

I taught geography and history to wealthy Indian girls in Calcutta for 19 years. I became the principal and the Mother Superior of the high school.

Then one day, I was called by God to help the poorest of the poor, "not only in the slums of Calcutta but all over the world." So, at the age of 37, I left the Sisters of Loreto. I removed my black veil and habit, and put on a white sari with three blue stripes. I pinned a small cross on my left shoulder, slipped into open sandals, and with five rupees—less than a dollar—walked into my new life.

HUMANITARIAN

On my first day of teaching the poor, I knelt on the ground and wrote the letters of the alphabet in the dirt with a stick. The children were curious about what I was doing and, slowly, my classes grew. Soon, many of my former students joined me and I founded a new order of nuns. Each girl had to take the three vows I had taken, plus one more: to serve wholeheartedly the poorest of the poor. This vow of the Missionaries of Charity sets us apart from all other orders of nuns.

There are 3 million homeless people in Calcutta. Many of them die on the streets, uncared-for and unloved. I opened a home for people who were dying so they would die surrounded by love and kindness. I opened orphanages to care for babies and children who had no parents, and tried to find homes for them so every child would feel loved. I fed the hungry and found shelter for the poor. I cared for people with leprosy, a terrible disease which causes parts of the body to appear to rot away.

In 1979, I received one of the world's greatest honors—the Nobel Peace Prize. The Nobel Prize committee said hunger and poverty can lead to war and that my efforts to fight both made the world a more peaceful place. I convinced the committee to cancel the celebration dinner and to use the money they would have spent to feed the hungry instead. I used the prize money I received—almost $200,000—to feed the poor and build homes for the homeless.

I died at the age of 87. I am buried in a corner of my convent in Calcutta. Today, more than 4,000 religious brothers and sisters of the Missionaries of Charity continue my work with the poorest of the poor all over the world. During my life, there were people who disagreed with my strict religious beliefs and the way I ran my order. But I always followed my beliefs. I did my work with love, believing "every act of love is a work of peace, no matter how small." You can help spread peace, too, if you will remember, "Peace begins with a smile."

COSTUME/PROPS

White sari with a border of three blue stripes

A small crucifix on left shoulder

Sandals

NOTES/TIPS FOR PRESENTERS

Mother Teresa's birth name is pronounced: AHG-nes GOHN-ja boh-yahd-JEE-zoo. To hear an audio file of this, go to the Voice of America Pronunciation website: <http://www.voa.gov/pronunciations>

Point out sari and crucifix when mentioned during presentation.

Mother Teresa would have an accent when speaking English. She would speak slowly.

End presentation with a smile.

Point out Albania, Ireland, and India on a map.

SUGGESTED RESOURCES

Chawla, Navin. *Mother Teresa: The Authorized Biography.* Rockport, MA: Element Books, 1996.

Dills, Tracey E. *Mother Teresa.* Broomall, PA: Chelsea House Publishing, 2001.

Sebba, Anne. *Mother Teresa: Beyond the Image.* New York: Doubleday, 1997.

Spink, Kathryn. *Mother Teresa: A Complete Authorized Biography.* San Francisco, CA: HarperCollins, 1997.

Stone, Elaine Murray. *Mother Teresa.* Mahwah, NJ: Paulist Press, 1999.

Biography: Mother Teresa: A Life of Devotion. Dir. Kevin Burns and Lawrence Williams. VHS. A&E Home Video, 1999.

Mother Teresa. Dir. Ann Petrie and Jeanette Petrie. VHS. Tapeworm, 1997.

Mother Teresa: Angel of Mercy. CNN Interactive. <http://www.cnn.com/WORLD/9709/mother.teresa/>.

HARRIET TUBMAN

HARRIET TUBMAN (1820 OR 1821–1913)

On my underground

railroad, I never ran

my train off the track.

And I never lost a

passenger.

(Reading "Wanted" poster): "Reward—$40,000 for capture of escaped slave known as Harriet Tubman." That's me. I made my way to freedom and helped hundreds of other slaves get away. But, that's the middle of my story. Let me start at the beginning.

I was born a slave in Maryland in 1820 or '21. My parents were Ben and Harriet Ross. We were the property of a plantation owner named Edward Brodas. My parents named me Araminta, but I later took my mother's name, Harriet. We lived in a cabin with a dirt floor and no furniture. I remember sleeping on hay piled on the floor with my feet in the ashes of our cooking fire to keep them warm.

When I was small, two of my sisters were sold to a slave trader. I never forgot the helpless, terrified looks on their faces as they were dragged away. We never saw them again.

I never went to school. I was put to work when I was 6 years old, doing household chores. When I was 7, Mr. Brodas hired me out to a woman who had me do housework all day long. Then she had me rock her baby all night. If I fell asleep, the baby cried and woke its mother. Then she'd beat me.

Later, Mr. Brodas had me work outdoors. Sometimes, I worked alongside my father. When we worked in the forest cutting trees, my father pointed out plants you could eat and plants you could use as medicine. He also taught me how to walk very quietly through the woods.

One day, I tried to help a slave who was running away. The overseer in charge of the slaves threw a heavy weight at the slave to stop him, but it hit me instead—right here. *(Point to forehead.)* I almost died. It left me with a dent in my forehead and I would often fall asleep for no reason.

When I was 23, Mr. Brodas allowed me to marry John Tubman, a free black man. I wanted John to run away with me, but he refused. So I stayed. But a few years later, I found out I was going to be sold. I knew I had to escape right away. There was a woman

ABOLITIONIST

who I thought helped runaway slaves, so I went to her house. She gave me food and told me how to get to another safe place.

I had heard rumors about an "Underground Railroad" that helped slaves escape to freedom. I discovered it wasn't really a railroad after all. It was a network of people helping slaves find their way to freedom in the north. I traveled on this network, staying in the shadows and sometimes wading in rivers so I wouldn't be tracked and captured.

I made my way safely north and settled in Philadelphia where I found work as a cook. I saved every penny I made so I could go back and rescue other slaves. But in 1850, the government passed the Fugitive Slave Act. This law said runaway slaves living anywhere in the United States could be returned to their owners, and anyone helping them escape could go to jail. Runaways had to go all the way to Canada—another 400 miles—to be safe.

The possibility of being returned to slavery didn't stop me from going back and leading more people to freedom. On my first trip, I rescued my sister, Mary, and her family. After that, I made two trips a year to Maryland. Wherever I went, I saw "wanted" posters with huge rewards for my capture. But I knew places where we could hide and not be found. We often waded neck-deep in icy streams to escape the men and the bloodhounds looking for us. In 10 years, I made 19 trips and rescued over 300 slaves without being caught.

In 1861, the Civil War began. I worked for the Union army, both as a nurse and as a spy. Once, I even led a raid in South Carolina that freed 800 slaves. But when the war ended, the army refused to pay me because I was a woman. After that, I joined Susan B. Anthony in the women's rights movement.

I lived to be 93 years old. During my life, I braved every obstacle to lead people to freedom. There were many dangers along the way, but "on my underground railroad, I never ran my train off the track. And I never lost a passenger."

COSTUME/PROPS

Simple, mid-to-late-19th century style dress or skirt and blouse

Men's trousers and jacket (when working for the Union Army)

"Wanted" poster

NOTES/TIPS FOR PRESENTERS

Tubman always carried a revolver and was not afraid to use it. She often threatened the fugitives that were traveling with her if they got "cold feet" and wanted to turn back. She feared they would turn her in, as well as other people, both black and white, who had helped them by providing food, shelter and transportation.

Tubman made Auburn, New York, her home in 1857. From 1896 to 1908, she worked to establish a retirement home there for poor black people. It became her final residence.

SUGGESTED RESOURCES

Bentley, Judith. *Harriet Tubman.* New York: Franklin Watts, 1990.

McClard, Megan. *Harriet Tubman: Slavery and the Underground Railroad.* Englewood Cliffs, NJ: Silver Burdett Press, 1991.

Rowley, John. *Harriet Tubman.* Des Plaines, IL: Heinemann Interactive Library, 1998.

Schraff, Anne E. *Harriet Tubman: Moses of the Underground Railroad.* Rev. ed. Berkeley Heights, NJ: Enslow Publishers, Inc., 2001.

Sullivan, George. *Harriet Tubman.* In Their Own Words Series. New York: Scholastic, Inc., 2001.

Taylor, M. W. *Harriet Tubman: Antislavery Activist.* New York: Chelsea House Publishers, 1991.

Harriet Tubman: Antislavery Activist. The Black Americans of Achievement Video Collection. VHS. Schlessinger Media, 1992.

Celebrate Black History Month. The History Channel. <http://www.historychannel.com/exhibits/blackhist/>.

National Women's Hall of Fame. <http://www.greatwomen.org>.

MADAM C. J. WALKER

MADAM C. J. WALKER
(1867–1919)

I have built my own

factory on my own

ground.

By dreaming of success and working hard, I started a business with $1.50 in my pocket and became a millionaire. I was the first American woman to do that. My name is Madam C. J. Walker.

When I was born, my parents named me Sarah—Sarah Breedlove. That was in 1867, shortly after the Civil War. We were sharecroppers on a plantation in Louisiana where my parents had been slaves. Life wasn't much different from slavery times. Even though I was just a little girl, I worked alongside my parents in the cotton fields from sunrise to sunset. I remember the sharp cotton bolls cutting my fingers as I picked cotton. Our shack had no windows, no water, no toilet and a dirt floor.

By the time I was 7, both my parents had died and I lived with my married sister. At 14, I got married to escape my sister's cruel husband. When my husband died, "I was left a widow at the age of twenty with a little girl to raise." We moved to St. Louis, Missouri, where there were better job opportunities for me and better schools for my daughter, Lelia (LEEL-yah). I found work cooking and doing laundry for white people to support Lelia and send her to college.

I always had money worries and I started losing my hair. This problem was common among black women back then. It was caused by stress, poor diet and damaging hair care products. One night, I had a strange dream in which an old man showed me how to mix a formula to save my hair. Some of the ingredients were grown in Africa and I sent for them. I mixed up the old man's formula and, when I tried it, my hair started growing. Some people say I really learned the recipe from another woman who sold hair products, but I think *my* story is better, don't you?

When my friends saw how good my hair looked, they asked to try my formula. It helped them, too, and they wanted more. I realized I could probably earn a living by making and selling the formula.

In 1906, I was living in Denver, Colorado, and I married a newspaperman named C. J. Walker. Using his initials and the title "Madam"—that was the custom for businesswomen back then—I

Profiles of Women Past & Present

ENTREPRENEUR, PHILANTHROPIST

became known as Madam C. J. Walker. With $1.50 in savings, I started my hair preparation company. My first product was "Madam Walker's Wonderful Hair Grower," which I sold door to door. My husband's knowledge of advertising and mail order procedures helped me increase my sales.

I traveled around the country training black women to sell my products, and my business grew. Lelia ran the mail order operation back at home. I hired black women to work in my factories and to teach the Walker Method in the beauty school I started. I opened beauty parlors in the United States, the Caribbean and South America—wherever black women lived. My laboratories and factories had the most modern equipment available. By 1916, 20,000 people were working for my company. I encouraged girls and women to make their own opportunities for success. My company helped by offering well-paid jobs and careers for black women.

My wealth made it possible for me to help improve the lives of women and African Americans in many ways. I donated thousands of dollars to schools, charitable organizations and political causes. Once, I helped organize a silent protest march of 10,000 people against lynching. As I told my agents, "This is the greatest country under the sun. But we must not let our love of country… cause us to stop our protest against wrong and injustice."

When I spoke at the National Negro Business League convention in 1912, I said, "I am a woman who came from the cotton fields of the South. I was promoted from there to the washtub. Then I was promoted to the cook kitchen. And from there I promoted myself into the business of manufacturing hair goods and preparations.… I have built my own factory on my own ground."

When asked the secret of my success, I said, "There is no royal flower-strewn path to success.… If I have accomplished anything in life it is because I have been willing to work hard."

When I died in 1919 at age 51, I left most of my fortune to the causes I had supported during my lifetime.

COSTUME/PROPS

Dark suit with long skirt or long black skirt and white blouse

Satchel for products, jars and bottles

Order book

NOTES/TIPS FOR PRESENTERS

Walker and her agents often wore black skirts and white blouses to call on clients.

Have you ever thought of starting a business? What kind of business would be interesting to you and why?

Sharecropping was common after the Civil War. Rather than sell their land, plantation owners would rent plots to family farmers in exchange for a share of the crop.

After the Civil War, lynching was used to terrorize people to make them too afraid to exercise their rights as American citizens. Members of white supremacist groups often kidnapped, tortured and killed black people, and law officials did nothing to stop them. Lynching continued in the U.S. for 100 years.

After her mother's death, Lelia changed her name to A'Lelia Walker and became a patroness of the arts during the Harlem Renaissance.

SUGGESTED RESOURCES

Bundles, A'Lelia. *On Her Own Ground: The Life and Times of Madam C. J. Walker.* New York: Scribner, 2001.

Bundles, A'Lelia Perry. *Madam C. J. Walker: Entrepreneur.* Philadelphia, PA: Chelsea House, 1991.

Lasky, Kathryn. *Vision of Beauty: The Story of Sarah Breedlove Walker.* Cambridge, MA: Candlewick Press, 2000.

McKissack, Patricia C. and Frederick McKissack. *Madam C. J. Walker: Self-Made Millionaire.* Hillside, NJ: Enslow Publishers, 1992.

Yanuzzi, Della A. *Madam C. J. Walker: Self-Made Businesswoman.* Berkeley Heights, NJ: Enslow Publishers, Inc., 2002.

Madam C. J. Walker. The Black Americans of Achievement Video Collection. VHS. Schlessinger Media, 1992.

Bundles, A'Lelia. *Madam C. J. Walker.* <http://www.madamcjwalker.com/>.

National Women's Hall of Fame. <http://www.greatwomen.org/>.

IDA B. WELLS-BARNETT

Ida B. Wells-Barnett (1862–1931)

There must always be a remedy for wrong and injustice if we only know how to find it.

I was born a slave in 1862 during the Civil War. After the war, we were free—free to live and work where we wanted, free to be treated fairly and free to get an education. You see, under slavery, those things were against the law. But after the Civil War, laws were made guaranteeing black Americans the same rights as white Americans. Many people ignored the laws, however, and black people suffered many injustices. My name is Ida B. Wells-Barnett, and I spent my life crusading to end injustice.

When the Freedmen's Aid Society came to my home town, Holly Springs, Mississippi, I enrolled in the school they started. After I learned to read, I often read newspapers to my father and his friends, and listened as they discussed politics and current events.

When I was 16, my parents and baby brother died in a yellow fever epidemic. After that, it was up to me to take care of my five younger sisters and brothers. I put on long skirts, put my hair up in a bun to look older and got a job teaching in a one-room schoolhouse. In 1884, I moved to Memphis, Tennessee, where I found another teaching job and attended college. By then, my sisters and brothers were living with relatives.

I often rode the train to work, and always sat in the "Ladies' Car." One day, the conductor came along and told me to move to the smoking car, the only place he would allow black people to ride. I said, "No," and two men pushed me off the train at the next stop. I sued the railroad company and won $500.

I wrote an article about my experience to encourage others to stand up for their rights, as I had done. That article was published by the black press—newspapers owned by black people. At that time, the black press was the only source of true information about black people and their lives. Many people liked my article and I was asked to write more. I wrote under a pen name—"Iola"—and became famous throughout the country.

Later, I became the editor and part owner of the Memphis *Free Speech and Headlight*. I wrote against injustice. Often, that made people angry. When I criticized the Memphis school board

ANTI-LYNCHING CRUSADER, JOURNALIST

for not giving black children as good an education as white children, they fired me from my teaching job.

I also wrote about lynching. Sometimes, white people who didn't want black people to have equal rights made up stories, saying a black person had committed a horrible crime. Then, they would get a crowd of people so angry that they would kill the black person. When three of my friends were lynched, I wrote an angry article against lynching. It made some people so furious that they burned down my newspaper office and threatened to kill me. Fortunately, I was away at the time and wasn't hurt. But I took the threats seriously and didn't return to Memphis.

I moved to New York and, over the next few years, I learned everything I could about lynching. I wrote many articles and traveled across the country, lecturing and helping organize anti-lynching campaigns. My research is still considered the best source of information about lynching.

Later, I moved to Chicago, where I met Ferdinand L. Barnett, a civil rights lawyer. We got married in 1895. I loved caring for the four children we had, but I couldn't stop working to end injustice. When I had to travel, the youngest baby often came with me.

I was one of two women who helped found the National Association for the Advancement of Colored People—the NAACP. But when the organization wouldn't take a strong enough stand against lynching, I resigned. I worked for woman suffrage—the right of women to vote—and started a suffrage organization for black women. In 1913, I marched in front of the White House with women from all over the country, demanding votes for women. I was harshly criticized when I walked with the white women from my state of Illinois. But I would not separate myself because of race.

I believed "there must always be a remedy for wrong and injustice if we only know how to find it." All my life, I searched for those remedies. People still remember me as a crusader against lynching and injustice, and a founder of the Civil Rights Movement.

COSTUME/PROPS

Young Ida:

Victorian style dress

Hair worn in a bun on top of head

Older Ida:

Matronly, 1920s style skirt and blouse

White hair, pulled back

NOTES/TIPS FOR PRESENTERS

Wells-Barnett handled herself with gentility and grace, as well as forthright determination.

When Wells-Barnett marched in the Woman Suffrage Parade in Washington, D.C., she was asked to march in a segregated section with other black women so the white suffragists from southern states would not be offended. She refused and marched, instead, with the white suffragists from Illinois.

Act out the Wells-Barnett skit in *Take a Walk in Their Shoes* by Glennette Turner.

Discuss or write journal entries from episodes in Wells-Barnett's life, such as being pushed off the train because she refused to sit in a separate car, being forced to flee her home because her life was threatened or not being able to vote because she was a woman.

Draw posters announcing Wells-Barnett's speeches about lynching.

SUGGESTED RESOURCES

Fradin, Dennis B. and Judith B. Fradin. *Ida B. Wells: Mother of the Civil Rights Movement.* New York: Clarion Books, 2000.

Lisandrelli, Elaine S. *Ida B. Wells-Barnett: Crusader Against Lynching.* Springfield, NJ: Enslow Publishers, Inc., 1998.

McKissack, Pat. *Ida B. Wells-Barnett: A Voice Against Violence.* Rev. ed. Berkeley Heights, NJ: Enslow Publishers, 2001.

Sterling, Dorothy. *Black Foremothers: Three Lives.* 2nd ed. New York: The Feminist Press, 1988.

Turner, Glennette Tilley. *Take a Walk in Their Shoes.* New York: Cobblehill Books/Dutton, 1989.

Ida B. Wells: A Passion for Justice. Dir. William Greaves. VHS. William Greaves Productions, 1990.

Celebrate Black History Month. The History Channel. <http://www.historychannel.com/exhibits/blackhist/>.

National Women's Hall of Fame. <http://www.greatwomen.org>.

CHIEN-SHIUNG WU

CHIEN-SHIUNG WU
(1912–1997)

Do you know what atoms are? Everything around you is made of atoms—the air you breathe, the water you drink, even you! Atoms are so tiny you can't see them without a special microscope. Atoms are made of even smaller particles—electrons spinning around a core called a nucleus. The study of the nucleus and the particles it is made of is called nuclear physics. My name is Dr. Chien-Shiung Wu (chyen schwen woo) and I am a nuclear physicist.

When I was born in China in 1912, most people there believed girls should not go to school. But my father didn't agree, and he opened the first school for girls where we lived. He encouraged my interest in science and math, and helped me prepare to go to college and have a career.

In high school, I studied to be a teacher. But I realized some students were learning more about science than I was. So, I borrowed their books and taught myself mathematics, chemistry and physics. Physics—the science of matter and energy—was my favorite subject and, somehow, I knew I would go on with that in college.

When I graduated from college, World War II was just beginning and China was at war with Japan. I wanted the best education possible, so I went to the United States—which hadn't entered the war yet—to study advanced physics at the University of California at Berkeley. Important physicists from all over the world were working there, and I studied with some of them. One of my teachers was Ernest Lawrence, who invented the cyclotron—also called the "atom-smasher."

By the time I earned my doctorate degree in 1940, I was known for my ability to design experiments and for my careful, accurate measurements. I was well qualified to teach physics at a top university, but Smith College, a school for women, was the only one willing to hire me. Later, I was the first woman hired to teach at Princeton University, which only admitted men at that time.

Before World War II ended, I joined a group of scientists doing war-related work at Columbia University in New York. When the war ended, I got a job as a researcher. And I had a baby boy

Nuclear Physicist

with my husband, who was also a physicist. I was lucky to have three things that allowed me to continue my work: a supportive husband, a home close to work and a good baby sitter. After all, "there is only one thing worse than coming home from the laboratory to a sink full of dishes, and that is not going to the laboratory at all!"

One day, a young physicist named Tsung-Dao Lee (zoong dow lee) came to my office with a problem. He and his partner, Chen-Ning Yang (young), said the results of some of their experiments didn't agree with an important law of physics. I told them to find out everything they could about that law. What they found was that no one had ever done experiments to prove whether the law was correct or not.

Lee and Yang needed someone to conduct an experiment to test their theory. "I could not pass up the chance to prove or disprove a basic law of nature." They suggested an experiment, and I figured out how to do it. I worked at Columbia and also in a laboratory in Washington, D.C., where the materials I was using could be chilled to extremely low temperatures. I repeated the experiment many times to be sure of my results. My experiment proved, without any doubt, that the law was not correct. Other scientists repeated the experiment and verified my result, but I was the first to do it.

Drs. Lee and Yang received the 1957 Nobel Prize for Physics for their work. Many people believe their Nobel Prize should have been shared with me. I had worked just as hard as they had on my experiment that proved their theory. Later, I received many other awards for my work, including the National Medal of Science.

After I retired from teaching and researching, I traveled, lectured and encouraged women to become scientists. Someone once asked me if I had any advice for students. I said, "Work as a scientist. Ask the right questions, keep good notes and try to understand things clearly." And remember, "science is not static but ever-growing and dynamic. … It is the courage to doubt what has long been established … that pushes the wheel of science forward."

COSTUME/PROPS

A cheongsam (Chinese dress) with trousers underneath or a white lab coat

Hair pulled back into a bun

NOTES/TIPS FOR PRESENTERS

Wu spoke slowly and precisely. She always felt more comfortable in Chinese dress, even after all her years in the United States.

The law of physics that Wu's experiment disproved in 1956 is Conservation of Parity. Formulated in 1925, it "implies that Nature is symmetrical and makes no distinction between right- and left-handed rotations, or between opposite sides of a subatomic particle." (American Physical Society. *APS News Online*. Dec. 2001. <http://www.aps.org/apsnews/1201/120107.html>.)

Discuss what Wu meant when she said, "Science is not static but ever-growing and dynamic.... It is the courage to doubt what has long been established... that pushes the wheel of science forward."

SUGGESTED RESOURCES

Kass-Simon, G. and Patricia Farnes, eds. *Women of Science: Righting the Record.* Bloomington, IN: Indiana University Press, 1990.

McGrayne, Sharon B. *Nobel Prize Women in Science.* New York: Birch Lane Press, 1993.

Stille, Darlene R. *Extraordinary Women Scientists.* Chicago: Children's Press, 1995.

Warren, Rebecca L. and Mary H. Thompson. *The Scientist Within You: Experiments and Biographies of Distinguished Women in Science.* Volume 1. 2nd ed. Eugene, OR: ACI Publishing, 1996.

Yount, Lisa. *Asian-American Scientists.* New York: Facts on File, Inc., 1998.

Contributions of 20th Century Women to Physics. UCLA. <http://www.physics.ucla.edu/~cwp>. (Click Search the Archive, then search for Wu.)

National Women's Hall of Fame. <http://www.greatwomen.org/>.

SUSAN B. ANTHONY
(1820–1906)

Imagine that you have a job—any job—like walking your neighbor's dog. Suppose that when payday arrives your neighbor says, "Here's your money. But because you're a girl, I'm not paying you as much as I would pay a boy." Is that fair? Of course not! I spent my life fighting unfairness. I am Susan B. Anthony.

When I was born in 1820, women weren't allowed to keep the money they earned, go to college or vote. My parents believed girls and boys were equals. They taught me to get a good education, work hard and try to end unfairness in the world.

When I grew up, I became a teacher. But I wasn't paid as much as the men who were teachers. I thought that was unfair! I believed I should receive "equal pay for equal [work]."

Later, I decided not to be a teacher anymore. I wanted to spend all my time working to end unfairness. I became an abolitionist. That means I worked to abolish, or end, slavery. Can you imagine? Americans owned other people and treated them like farm animals. I wanted to stop that.

In 1851, I met Elizabeth Cady Stanton, a woman who was working for women's rights. We became friends and worked together for the right of women to vote. I traveled all over the United States giving speeches that Elizabeth and I wrote. I told audiences why women should be allowed to vote. Many times, the people in the audience believed women shouldn't make speeches. They also disagreed with me. So they'd boo or call me names. But I didn't care what people thought. I just worked harder.

One time, I was arrested and put on trial for voting in an election for President of the United States. After all, I was a citizen of the United States. Didn't that give me the right to vote? The judge decided I was guilty before my trial started.

I made my last speech when was I was 86 years old. There were many young women in the audience and I told them to keep fighting for the right of women to vote. I said, "Failure is impossible." Several weeks later, I died.

It took 14 more years for women to win the right to vote. In 1920, the 19th Amendment to the U.S. Constitution, also called the Susan B. Anthony Amendment, gave women the right to vote. I'm proud to say I helped win the right to vote for all the women who came after me.

ANN BANCROFT
(1955–   )

Do you know where the North Pole is? It's at the top of the world. I've been there. I've been to the South Pole and Antarctica, too. I'm Ann Bancroft and I'm a polar explorer.

When I was growing up, I knew "I wanted to be 'the first' to do something special." I lived in Minnesota and I loved being outside during the cold, snowy days of winter. Sometimes, I'd pull my sled across the snowy fields near my house and pretend I was far away exploring a place where no one had ever been before.

I also loved backpacking and camping and climbing and, when I grew up, I climbed Mount McKinley in Alaska. It's so tall, it's like climbing from your backyard to an airplane you can hardly see in the sky.

After that, I met a man who was leading a dogsled team to the North Pole and I asked if I could go along. When I told him I could ski and hike, he said, "Yes, but you'll be the only woman on the trip."

During our trip, we lived without heat or electricity or running water. Everyone wore warm coats, even when we slept. Sometimes, my face froze because it was so cold—even colder than the freezer in your refrigerator. We traveled 1,000 miles in 55 days, and I became the first woman to reach the North Pole by dogsled.

I was so excited that all I could think about was making another trip, this time to the South Pole with a team of women only—no men and no dogs.

As we skied to the South Pole, we each pulled a sled piled high with 200 pounds of supplies. That's like pulling your parents on an icy road. We traveled for two months and one week, and became the "first all women's group" to ski to the South Pole. We were the happiest women in the world. Of course, I was ready for another adventure.

Eight years later, Liv (leev) Arnesen and I became the first women ever to ski 1,900 miles across the continent of Antarctica. During our 93-day journey, we had no chairs to sit on, we didn't see any other people and we couldn't take showers. But we didn't mind because we were doing what we loved most.

I've never loved anything more than stepping onto snow that has never been stepped on before. So, the next time you fall on fresh snow to make your snow angel, close your eyes and think of yourself as an explorer like me. And then know that whatever your special dream is, someday you'll be telling your story of how you made it come true.

MARGARET BOURKE-WHITE (1904–1971)

Can you imagine not having television? How would you learn about the news? Well, you might read a newspaper, or listen to the radio, but it would be hard to *see* historic events unless you were right where they were happening. But if someone traveled all over the world and took pictures of historic events for magazines and books, you *would* be able to see them. That's what I did. I traveled across the United States and around the world taking photos of historic events before there was television. I'm Margaret Bourke-White.

When I was your age, sometimes I pretended to take pictures, using an empty box as my camera. Then, when I was 8, my father took me to a factory and I saw how machine parts were made. It was exciting! I wished I could capture what I was seeing with a real camera to show my friends.

You might think I studied photography when I started college, but I didn't. It was hard for me to decide what I wanted to study because I was interested in so many things. I even thought about being a herpetologist—a scientist who studies reptiles and snakes. But by the time I graduated, I knew I would earn my living as a photographer because I wanted to "share the things I saw and learned."

One time, I photographed two little girls who were twins. They were so poor that they shared the only coat and pair of shoes they owned. That's why they had to take turns going to school. When people saw my pictures of the girls, they wanted to do something to help the poor.

Later, I worked for a magazine called *Life*. One of my pictures was on the cover of the very first issue of *Life*. Inside, I used photographs to tell a story in a photo essay. I was the first person to do that.

During World War II, I was the first woman to take photographs during battles. I had to sleep on the ground and wash myself with water scooped up in my helmet, just like the soldiers did. I crawled through muddy fields with the soldiers and jumped into holes in the ground when the enemy started shooting at us. I was in danger, but while I was taking pictures, I didn't notice anything else around me—even the danger.

My mother always told me to "open all the doors" and, for 25 years, I did just that. I got the stories no one else got, and I got them first.

EUGENIE CLARK
(1922–   )

Oh, hello! Please excuse my appearance. I just got back from a dive to study eels on the sandy floor of the Red Sea. I'm Dr. Eugenie Clark.

When I was growing up in New York City, my favorite place to go was the aquarium. I spent hours staring into tanks containing all kinds of fish. My favorite was the shark. Oh, how I wanted to swim with that shark!

When I was 9, my mother bought me an aquarium. Soon, I had a large collection of fish. When I grew up and went to college, I decided to be an ichthyologist—a scientist who studies fish.

After college, I went to California and worked at a marine laboratory, a place where scientists study ocean life. While I was there, I learned to dive. The first time I went deep into the ocean, the air tube connected to my helmet leaked. Suddenly, I couldn't breathe! Luckily, I didn't get hurt, but it was scary.

Later, I traveled to the tiny islands of Micronesia in the Pacific Ocean to learn about poisonous fish. I traveled from island to island—diving, collecting fish and making friends. One day while I was diving, a big shark swam right by me. At that moment, I remembered wishing I could swim with the shark when I was a girl. Now I had done it!

When I got back home, I wrote a book about my adventures. Some people who lived in Florida read it and asked me to help them start a marine laboratory. Of course, I said yes. The lab grew quickly. We had a big underwater pen to hold live sharks. I studied the sharks closely and learned they are smart and gentle.

One time, I went to Mexico to study "sleeping" sharks in an underwater cave. Like most people, I thought sharks had to swim all the time to breathe and didn't sleep. I discovered the sharks could breathe without swimming in the underwater cave because there was extra oxygen in the water. So the sharks weren't asleep, they were just resting.

I'm not afraid of sharks. I *was* bitten once, but it happened while I was driving my car. I stopped suddenly and a shark jaw on the seat next to me fell against my arm. The teeth cut me, but it didn't hurt very much.

"I plan to keep diving and researching… until I'm 90 years old." I'm lucky I've been able to do what I love for so many years. I hope as you grow up, you'll find something you love to do and have the chance to do it your whole life.

Jerrie Cobb
(1931–   )

Imagine you're flying high up in the sky and you're in control. You know what every black switch and every red button is for, and you can steer left and right, and up and down, too. This is what I do. My name is Jerrie Cobb and I'm a pilot.

When I was 12, my father took me for a ride in his airplane and I fell in love with flying. When I was 16, I got my pilot's license and flew "solo"—or by myself— for the first time. When I grew up, I decided to be a pilot.

The jobs I took were so dangerous that most men didn't want them. For one job, I flew airplanes to Peru in South America. I had to fly across shark-filled oceans, thick green jungles and high mountains to reach my destination.

I became one of the world's best pilots, setting many speed, distance and altitude records. I was such a good pilot that NASA—the National Aeronautics and Space Administration—asked me to take special tests to see if I would make a good astronaut. They spun me around, tilted me in special machines and dropped me into water. I did better than almost everyone who took the tests—even the men—and qualified to be America's first woman astronaut.

NASA asked me to be part of a team of women astronauts called the Mercury 13. But later, NASA decided not to send women into space after all. It would be a long time before American women became astronauts. I was very disappointed, but I didn't give up my dream of rocketing into space.

I decided to use my love of flying for a new purpose—to help people living in the Amazon jungle of South America. The people there are very poor. They live in small huts, and many are sick and hungry. It's hard to reach them by land because they live far into the jungle, but I can get there by plane. I take them seeds and medicines and lots of love. I also fly them to hospitals when they're too sick for me to help them.

Except for my plane, I work alone. I return to the United States only once a year. The jungle is my home, and the native people are my friends and family. I eat, sleep, work and share my life with them. For my work in the Amazon, I was nominated for the Nobel Peace Prize in 1981.

There's only one thing that would take me away from my work in the Amazon jungle—the chance to go into space. "Nothing means more to me." I am over 70 years old, but I'll never give up my dream of rocketing into space.

AGNES DE MILLE
(1905–1993)

Have you ever seen a play where the actors sing and dance? That kind of play is called a musical. The person who creates the dances in a musical is called the choreographer. That's what I did. I'm Agnes de Mille.

I always loved to dance. When I was a little girl, I would whirl around for anyone who cared to watch me. When I was 9, my family moved from New York to California. My uncle was a famous movie director and he asked my father, who wrote plays, to come and work with him.

Sometimes, my sister, Margaret, and I were excused from school to watch movies being filmed. It was exciting! I dreamed of becoming an actress. Then, one day, Mother took me to see a famous ballerina. From that day on, I wanted to be a dancer.

When I was 14, my sister and I started ballet school. The teacher said I was too old to begin dancing. If you want to be a ballet dancer, you must begin when your body is growing. But I was determined to dance. I took dance lessons all through school and in college, too.

After I finished college, we moved back to New York. I studied dance and created my own dances. Then, I heard that a Russian ballet company was looking for a new ballet about America. I told them my idea of a cowgirl out to win the heart of a young cowboy and they liked it. A great American music composer named Aaron Copland wrote the music, and I created the dances. The ballet was called *Rodeo* (roh-DAY-oh). I told a story with the dances. I used horseback riding and roping movements.

On opening night, I danced the role of the cowgirl. If it is possible for a life to change at one given moment—that was my moment. Chewing gum and wearing a Texas hat, I did what I had been preparing for my whole life—I danced. The audience liked *Rodeo* so much, they called us back 22 times to take bows.

Suddenly, my life changed. Two famous song writers, Rodgers and Hammerstein, asked me to create the dances for a musical called *Oklahoma!* It was about farmers and ranchers in Oklahoma. It was a huge hit. Later, I choreographed other musicals for Rodgers and Hammerstein, including *Carousel* and *Brigadoon*. I also wrote many books about dance and my life.

I lived until I was 88 years old. I wanted people to remember me with just one word: "Dancer." Because, "to dance means to: step out on the great stages of the world, to flash and soar… to feel the magic work."

Profiles of Women Past & Present

FANNIE FARMER
(1857–1915)

Can you cook? Well, if you'd like to learn, just ask me. In my day, I was the most famous cooking teacher in the United States. My name is Fannie Farmer.

When I was your age, cooking was harder than it is now. We didn't have freezers and we didn't have microwaves. We did have stoves, but they didn't have buttons or dials to turn them on and off, and set the temperature. Instead, you built a fire inside the stove and changed the temperature by opening and closing vents to bring in cold air. Believe me, it wasn't easy.

I was born in 1857 in Boston, Massachusetts. I wanted to be a schoolteacher when I grew up but, before I finished high school, I got very sick and couldn't move my legs. It took me a long time to get better.

I thought I'd have to give up my dream of teaching because I didn't finish high school. Then, my sister said I should go to the Boston Cooking School and learn to be a cooking teacher. I thought that was funny because I wasn't a very good cook. When I baked cookies, I often burned them.

Well, I did go to the Boston Cooking School. After I finished, I taught my friends' daughters how to cook. One day, I showed them how to measure flour. *(Hold up spoon and demonstrate.)* For a rounded tablespoon, you fill the spoon to overflowing, then shake it gently until there's the same amount of flour rounded up above the spoon as there is in the spoon. One girl said, "If I do it that way, I might get it different every time. Why not use two level spoonfuls?"

She was right. From then on, I taught my students to measure level spoonfuls. I told them, "correct measurements are… necessary [for] the best results."

Later, I became a teacher—and then the principal—at the Boston Cooking School. I rewrote a cookbook and replaced all the rounded measurements with level ones. Then, I had my students try all the recipes to make sure they tasted good and that the instructions were correct. That book—*The Boston Cooking-School Cook Book*—was first published over a hundred years ago. Since then, other cooks have kept it up to date. It's still a best seller, but now it's called *The Fannie Farmer Cookbook*.

Later, I started my own cooking school—Miss Farmer's School of Cookery. I wanted my students to find enjoyment in preparing food for their families.

I never stopped teaching, even when I became ill again and had to use a wheelchair. I died in 1915. In my day, I was called "the Mother of Level Measurement."

DOLORES HUERTA
(1930–   )

My name is Dolores Huerta (HWAIR-tah) and I'm a political activist. I help people work together to make the world a better place.

My mother raised my sisters and brothers and me all by herself. It's not easy being a single parent and working all the time, but my mother taught me an important lesson in life—perseverance. Perseverance means you keep on trying, even when you can't do something the first time.

When I was a little girl, I took dance lessons and dreamed of being a dancer. But when I finished college, I decided to be a teacher, instead, because I wanted to help people. My students often came to school hungry and needing shoes. Their parents were farm workers and they were very poor.

"I thought I could do more by organizing farm workers than by trying to teach their hungry children." So, I left teaching and worked for a group of people who made sure Mexican-Americans got to vote in elections. Voting is a right held by every American citizen. When you vote, you have a say in how your government is run.

Then, I met a man named César Chávez. Together, we organized the United Farm Workers labor union. A labor union is a group of workers who join together to help each other get better working conditions. Can you imagine working all day and not being able to go to the bathroom or not having fresh water to drink, and not being able to do anything about it? That's what life was like for many farm workers before the union. The union helped the workers win many rights, because when everyone stands up together and demands change, people listen.

Several California grape growers—companies that owned farms that grew grapes—didn't want their workers to belong to the United Farm Workers union. I helped organize a strike against those companies. A strike is when everybody agrees to stop working in order to get what they want. It takes a lot of courage to strike, because you may not win and sometimes you even lose your job. The union members stopped picking grapes and many people stopped buying grapes. When people didn't buy grapes, the growers didn't make money. The strike ended when the growers let their workers join the union.

I'm proud that my children have grown up to be political activists like me. I expect all of my children and grandchildren and great-grandchildren to work together to build a better world. I expect all of you to do that, too. Do I believe it's possible to build a better world? "¡Sí, se puede!" (see say PWEH-they)—Yes, it can be done!

Profiles of Women Past & Present

SOR JUANA INÉS DE LA CRUZ (1648 OR 1651–1695)

When I was a little girl, I loved to learn. I never imagined that one day I would defend the right of women to think and learn. But when I grew up, I did that in my writing. I am Sor Juana Inés de la Cruz (sore HWAH-nah ee-NESS deh lah CREWTH)—Sister Juana Inés of the Cross.

I was born over 350 years ago in Mexico. In my grandfather's house, where I grew up, books were important. When I was just 3 years old, I followed my sister to school so I could learn to read. Later, I heard about a school in Mexico City where science was taught. But girls were not allowed to attend. I begged my mother to dress me as a boy and send me to that school, but she said no. So I learned about science—and many other things—from the books in my grandfather's library.

When I was 8, I went to Mexico City to live with my aunt and uncle. They were rich and lived in a fine house. My uncle was a friend of the viceroy, an important man sent by Spain to rule in Mexico. The viceroy's wife invited me to live at their palace. Life there was exciting! I went to plays, concerts and dances. I wrote poems to celebrate special events. I met interesting people and had many opportunities to learn.

But I wanted to do more with my life than live at the palace. I wanted to write and study. So, when I was 17, I became a nun and entered a special convent where I could do that. I lived in a cell—similar to what is now called an apartment. It had several rooms, including a library with many books.

I wasn't allowed to leave the convent, but people could visit me. I entertained friends with music and lively discussions. I wrote plays, poems and songs. In my writing, I spoke for slaves, Indians, women and others who were mistreated. I published three books of poetry and became famous.

Sometimes, people didn't approve of the things I wrote. The bishop in charge of the convent where I lived told me to write only about religious matters. I wrote him a long letter telling him I believed I should be able to decide for myself what I would write or learn about. But he didn't agree with me, so I stopped writing. I sold the books in my library and used the money to help poor people.

I stayed in the convent and died a year later when a terrible plague struck Mexico City. Even today, I am remembered as one of the greatest women poets of Mexico.

ELLEN OCHOA
(1958–   )

Have you ever wished you could travel in space? Well, I *have* traveled in space. I'm an astronaut. In fact, I was the first Mexican-American woman chosen to be an astronaut. I'm Dr. Ellen Ochoa (oh-CHO-ah).

When I was growing up, I always worked hard and did my best in school. My favorite subjects were math, English and music. I played the flute.

In college, I took lots of physics and engineering classes. In physics, I learned about things like motion, light and sound. In my engineering classes, I learned how to use science and math to figure out how to build things. By the time I finished college, I had earned a Ph.D. in engineering. That's how I became Dr. Ellen Ochoa.

Some of my college friends applied to NASA—the National Aeronautics and Space Administration—to become astronauts. I'd never thought about being an astronaut because, when I was growing up, all the astronauts were men. But NASA wanted women to be astronauts. And they wanted scientists! I knew I was qualified, so I applied. Several years later, NASA chose me to be an astronaut. I went to Houston, Texas, for astronaut training. I learned everything astronauts need to know.

One thing I learned about was being weightless. In space, astronauts don't walk—we float. To practice being weightless, we flew in a jet plane. The pilot flew the plane up and down like a roller coaster. When the plane went down, we were weightless. After my training, I was ready for a mission—a trip into space aboard the Space Shuttle.

So far, I've been to space four times. During my first two missions, I operated a robotic arm to launch satellites into space. The robotic arm is 50 feet long. It's not a real arm, but it has wrist, elbow and shoulder joints just like your arm has. I operated it with hand controllers—almost like the hand controllers you use for video games.

I've been on two missions to the ISS—the International Space Station. The ISS is a special laboratory in space where scientists from around the world live and work together. Both times I've been there, we docked with the ISS and delivered supplies. "It was exciting to look out at Earth from space. It was beautiful."

I hope you're excited about science, and maybe even thinking about being a scientist or an astronaut when you grow up. I had the opportunity to be an astronaut because I worked hard and got a good education. Remember, "a good education can take you anywhere on Earth and beyond."

MOTHER TERESA
(1910–1997)

My life began in a country called Albania. My family always called me Gonxha (GOHN-jah)—my middle name, which means "flower bud"—because I was plump and rosy. But most people know me as Mother Teresa.

I was a happy girl who loved to run and play games with my sister and brother. Often, I went with my mother to take food or money to people who had less than we had.

While I was growing up, Catholic missionaries would visit our little village and tell us about their work with poor people in India. This made a great impression on me. When I grew up, I decided to become a nun so I could help the poor and needy. I left my home and joined the Sisters of Loreto.

When I became a nun, I promised three things: to give up all possessions, to be pure in mind and body, and to obey my religious superiors. I chose a new name—Teresa—for St. Therese, who believed doing small things with love could be very important. That's how I became Mother Teresa.

I was sent to Calcutta, India, where I was a teacher for many years. But one day, I knew God had a new purpose for my life—to help the poorest of the poor by living and working among them. So, I removed my black nun's veil and clothing, put on a white sari with three blue stripes and stepped into my new life working with poor people in the streets of Calcutta. I started a new order of nuns called the Missionaries of Charity.

Millions of homeless people lived in Calcutta, many sick and dying. They had no one to care for them and no one to love them. There were also homeless babies and children with no parents. I opened orphanages so they would have a place to live and tried to find homes so every baby and child would feel wanted.

In 1979, I received one of the world's greatest honors—the Nobel Peace Prize. The people who gave me the prize said my work helped make the world a more peaceful place. I used the $200,000 prize money I received to feed the poor and build homes for the homeless.

I lived to be 87 years old. For 50 years, I gave food to the hungry, comfort to the sick and shelter to the homeless. I did my work with love because I believed "every act of love is a work of peace, no matter how small." You can help spread peace, too, if you will remember, "Peace begins with a smile."

HARRIET TUBMAN
(1820 OR 1821–1913)

(Reading "Wanted" poster): "Reward—$40,000 for capture of escaped slave known as Harriet Tubman." That's me. I made my way to freedom and helped many other slaves get away. But that's the middle of my story. Let me start at the beginning.

I was born a slave in Maryland in 1820 or '21. My parents were slaves, too. We were the property of Mr. Edward Brodas. My parents named me Araminta, but later I took my mother's name—Harriet. We lived in a cabin with a dirt floor and no furniture. I remember sleeping on hay piled on the floor with my feet in the ashes of our cooking fire to keep them warm.

I never went to school. When I was only 6 years old, I was put to work doing household chores. Later, I worked outdoors. Sometimes, I worked alongside my father, cutting trees in the forest. He pointed out plants you could eat or use as medicine, and taught me how to walk very quietly through the woods.

One day, I tried to help a slave who was running away. The man in charge of the slaves threw a heavy weight to stop him, and it hit me instead—right here. *(Point to forehead.)* I almost died. The deep scar on my forehead never went away.

When Mr. Brodas died, I knew I would be sold. I had to escape. I knew about a woman who might help runaway slaves, so I went to her house. She gave me food and directions to another safe place. I had heard stories about an Underground Railroad that helped slaves get away. Suddenly, I realized the Underground Railroad wasn't a real railroad—it was people who helped slaves travel to freedom in the north.

With the help of many people, I made my way safely to Philadelphia. I found a job as a cook and saved every penny so I could go back and help other slaves escape. My first trip back, I rescued my sister and her family. I went back many other times and led other slaves to freedom. I became well-known and many rewards were offered for my capture. But, I knew how to keep people from noticing me. When we traveled, we always stayed in the shadows. Sometimes, we waded in rivers so the men and the dogs that were looking for us wouldn't find us.

During my lifetime, I faced many dangers to lead people to freedom on the Underground Railroad. I made 19 trips and rescued over 300 slaves without ever being caught. Looking back, I can truthfully say, "On my underground railroad, I never ran my train off the track. And I never lost a passenger."

Madam C. J. Walker (1867–1919)

I had $1.50 in my pocket when I started my business. With lots of hard work, I turned it into a million dollars. I was the first woman in America to do that. But my life wasn't easy. Let me tell you my story.

My name is Sarah Breedlove Walker. My parents had been slaves, but in 1867—when I was born—they were free. When I was growing up in Louisiana, we all worked from sunrise to sunset, picking cotton. It was hard work. We lived in a shack with no windows, no water, no toilet and a dirt floor.

My life didn't get much better for many years. By the time I was 7 years old, my parents had died and I lived with my sister and her cruel husband. When I was 14, I got married. We had a baby girl and, when my husband died, "I was left a widow at the age of 20 with a little girl to raise." We moved to St. Louis, Missouri, where I found work cooking and washing clothes for white people. I didn't earn much money, but it was enough to support my daughter, Lelia, and send her to college.

I was very poor. Most of the time, I didn't have enough food to eat and I started losing my hair. One night, I had a strange dream. In the dream, an old man mixed up a formula to save my hair. I tried his formula and it worked. My hair started growing! My friends tried the formula and it helped them, too. I thought maybe I could earn a living by making and selling the formula.

I moved to Denver, Colorado, in 1905. Soon after that, I married C. J. Walker. I used his initials and added the title "Madam"—that was the custom for businesswomen back then—and became known as Madam C. J. Walker. I used my savings of $1.50 to start my hair preparation company. My first product was called "Madam Walker's Wonderful Hair Grower" and I sold it door to door.

I taught other women to sell my products door to door, and also in the beauty salons I opened in the U.S., the Caribbean and South America—wherever black women lived. My company provided good jobs and helped many women make their own opportunities for success. I used the money I earned to help improve the lives of women and African-Americans.

I was only 51 years old when I died. All my life, I worked hard to move into better and better jobs. Then, I "built my own factory on my own ground." I proved if you have faith in yourself and work hard, you can achieve success.

IDA B. WELLS-BARNETT (1862–1931)

I was born in 1862 during the Civil War. When the war ended, my family and all the other slaves were free. That meant my mother and father were paid for their work. It meant I could learn to read and write. My name is Ida B. Wells-Barnett.

When I was 16, my parents and baby brother died from yellow fever. After that, it was up to me to take care of my younger sisters and brothers. I got a job teaching in a one-room school house. Later, my sisters and brothers went to live with relatives and I moved to Memphis, Tennessee, where I found another teaching job.

I often rode a train to work and I always sat in a special car for women called the "Ladies' Car." One day, the conductor told me to move to the smoking car, the only place he would allow black people to ride. I said, "No," and two men pushed me off the train at the next stop. That was unfair! I decided to speak out and work to change things that I believed were unfair.

I wrote a newspaper article about what happened to me on the train. People liked my article and asked me to write more. Later, I became the editor and part owner of a newspaper called the *Free Speech and Headlight*. Sometimes, my articles made people angry. When I spoke out against the Memphis school board for not giving black children as good an education as white children, they fired me from my teaching job.

I often wrote about lynching. In those days, white people who didn't want black people to have equal rights sometimes made up stories, saying a black person had committed a horrible crime. Then, they would get a crowd of people so angry that they would kill the black person. This was called lynching. When three of my friends were killed this way, I wrote an angry article against lynching. It made some people so furious that they burned down the newspaper office and threatened to kill me. I was in so much danger that I left Memphis forever.

After that, I lived in New York and, later, in Chicago. In 1895, I married Ferdinand L. Barnett, a civil rights lawyer. Even after our four children were born, I kept on working to end unfairness. I worked for woman suffrage—the right of women to vote. I was one of two women who helped start the National Association for the Advancement of Colored People—the NAACP.

All my life, I spoke out against things I believed were unfair and said what I believed. People still remember me as a crusader against lynching and a founder of the Civil Rights Movement.

CHIEN-SHIUNG WU (1912–1997)

Do you know what atoms are? Everything around you is made of atoms—the air you breathe, the water you drink, even you! Atoms are so tiny you can't see them without a special microscope. Atoms are made of even smaller particles—electrons spinning around a center called the nucleus. Scientists who study the nucleus are called nuclear physicists. That's what I do. My name is Dr. Chien-Shiung Wu (chyen schwen woo).

When I was born in China in 1912, most people believed girls shouldn't go to school. But my father didn't agree. He opened the first school for girls where we lived, and helped me prepare to go to college and have a career. In high school, I studied math, chemistry and physics. Physics was my favorite subject. In physics, you study things like motion, light and sound.

After I finished college, I traveled to the United States to study physics at the University of California at Berkeley. It was an exciting place to be. Important physicists from all over the world were there, and I worked with them. I became very good at planning experiments and taking careful, correct measurements when I did them. Later, I used these skills as a researcher and teacher.

One day, a young physicist named Lee came to me with a problem. He and his partner, Yang (young), said the results of their experiments showed an important law of physics might be wrong. I told them to learn everything they could about that law. They found that no one had ever done experiments to prove whether it was right or wrong. Lee and Yang asked me to help them. I couldn't pass up the chance to prove or disprove a law of science, so I said yes.

Lee and Yang had an idea for an experiment and I figured out how to do it. I did the experiment and it proved—without any doubt—that the important law of physics was wrong. Other scientists did my experiment and got the same result, but I was the first to do it.

Drs. Lee and Yang received an important award for their work—the Nobel Prize for Physics. Many people believe I should have received the Nobel Prize, too. I worked just as hard as Lee and Yang did to prove that law of physics wrong. Later, I received many awards for my scientific work.

Someone once asked me if I had any advice for students. I said, "Ask the right questions, keep good notes and try to understand things clearly." All of these things will help you no matter what you decide to be when you grow up.

Appendix

SAMPLE LETTER TO SCHOOL DISTRICT

[Body of a letter to school superintendents, curriculum directors and/or school board members introducing "Profiles of Women Past & Present" and requesting approval to schedule classroom presentations. Send in January.]

In celebration of National Women's History Month in March, (name of organization) would like to provide students in your district the opportunity to meet women from history through a series of classroom "living history" presentations. For five consecutive days, volunteer presenters from (name of organization) will visit classrooms, in costume, portraying notable historic and contemporary women. The short presentations will be provided at no cost to the school district or to individual schools.

The women to be portrayed are: (list of women selected).

These presentations of "Profiles of Women Past & Present" will give your students the chance to meet remarkable women who overcame obstacles and reached the goals they set for themselves. They will discover the many important contributions women have made to our society. Girls will be provided with positive role models. Finally, all students will be introduced to the wealth of women's history.

With your approval, we will contact the principals at all elementary and/or intermediate schools in your district to schedule the presentations. Please contact (name and phone number of person coordinating presentations) if you have any questions.

SAMPLE LETTER TO SCHOOL PRINCIPALS

[Body of letter to school principals announcing "Profiles of Women Past & Present" and providing details about scheduling. Send as soon as possible after securing approval from the superintendent, curriculum director and/or school board. Copies of illustrations of the women to be portrayed, Enrichment Activities, Suggested Resources and an announcement flyer for teachers can be included with this letter. Send copy to superintendent, director of curriculum, and/or school board as a follow-up to the letter introducing the presentations.]

In celebration of National Women's History Month, (name of organization) will provide your students the opportunity to meet women from history through a series of five-minute classroom "living history" presentations during the week of (dates). For five consecutive days, we will provide volunteer presenters to visit your classrooms, in costume, portraying notable historic or contemporary women. The presentations will be provided at no cost to your school and will require no extra work by your teachers. We have obtained approval from (appropriate information) to schedule these presentations at your school.

The women to be portrayed are: (list of women selected).

The presenters assigned to your school will contact you directly no later than (date—about one month before presentations) to introduce themselves and to determine the best time for the presentations to be made. The number of classes will determine the amount of time needed at your school. Each day during the week of the classroom visits, the presenters will check in with you or your school secretary to see, before they begin, if there are any special considerations for that day. Please give your teachers a schedule for the week and let them know the presenters will wait to be acknowledged before beginning their presentations.

These presentations of "Profiles of Women Past & Present" will give your students the chance to meet remarkable women who overcame obstacles and reached the goals they set for themselves. The students will discover the many important contributions women have made to our society. Girls will be provided with positive role models. Finally, all students will be introduced to the wealth of women's history.

We thank you for your support of these presentations. Please contact (name and phone number of person coordinating presentations) if you have any questions.

SAMPLE LETTER TO CLASSROOM PRESENTERS

[Body of confirmation letter to presenters regarding contacts with their assigned school. Send after you have obtained appropriate school district approval, sent letters to principals and recruited the volunteer presenters. If the presenters are girls, you may want to adapt this letter.]

Thank you for volunteering to portray (_____ name of woman _____) at (_____ name of school _____) on (_____ date _____) as part of this year's presentations of "Profiles of Women Past & Present."

Please follow these procedures when contacting and making the presentations at your assigned school:

1. NO LATER than (date referred to in letter to principal), contact the principal or secretary at your school to introduce yourself and to determine the best time during the day for your presentations.

   Contact: (principal's name and phone number)

2. On the day of your presentation, check in with the principal or secretary when you arrive at the school to see if there are any special considerations for that day.

3. When entering each classroom, wait for the teacher to acknowledge your presence before beginning your presentation.

Thank you for taking time from your busy schedule to make women's history "come alive" for the students in our community. Please contact (name and phone number of person coordinating presentations) if you have any questions.

SAMPLE MEDIA RELEASE

[Send 2 to 3 weeks in advance to local newspapers and/or media. The format given is correct, but the body of the release should be double spaced.]

NEWS RELEASE
FOR IMMEDIATE RELEASE
DATE:　　　(date the release is submitted)
CONTACT:　(name and phone number of person coordinating presentations)

(name of organization) Volunteers to Present
"Profiles of Women Past & Present" at Local Schools

Members of (name of organization) will provide women's history presentations at local schools during the week of (dates) to celebrate National Women's History Month. Volunteers will visit classrooms, in costume, and portray notable historic and contemporary women. The women who will be portrayed are: (list of women to be portrayed).

These presentations of "Profiles of Women Past & Present" were initiated in 1987 by the American Association of University Women, Thousand Oaks (CA) Branch, to introduce students to the many important contributions women have made to society and to the wealth of women's history.

PUBLIC ACCESS TELEVISION TIPS

We have produced several videos of our annual Women's History Project presentations for broadcast on our local public access television station. This has made the presentations available to a wider audience and made our project more visible in our community. If you have a public access station, you might want to explore videotaping your presentation for broadcast.

Cable television companies are required, by law, to provide a public access channel and allow community members to produce programs or videotapes for broadcast. You will probably be required to submit a written application in advance to assure the company that you are not violating any copyrights. Contact your local cable television company for specific details.

For assistance videotaping your presentations, find out if there is a video club in your area, or check with your local university, community college or high school to see if they have a video program. Often, they are looking for events and programs to videotape.

If you produce a video, keep in mind that permission is granted to non-profit organizations or individuals to use the monologues in *Profiles of Women Past & Present* for non-commercial performances, as long as the American Association of University Women, Thousand Oaks California Branch, Inc., is credited with authorship.

SAMPLE ANNOUNCEMENT FLYER

Coming Soon!

Profiles of Women
Past & Present

WHAT: Classroom "visits" by notable women in history (each approximately five minutes in length with costumes and props):

(list of women to be portrayed, such as: Fannie Farmer, Cooking Teacher and Author; Chien-Shiung Wu, Nuclear Physicist; Agnes de Mille, Dancer and Choreographer; Dolores Huerta, Political Activist and Union Organizer; and Madam C. J. Walker, Entrepreneur and Philanthropist)

WHY: To introduce students to important contributions women have made to society and to the wealth of women's history

WHO: (name of organization)

WHEN: (date of presentations)

WHERE: (name of school)

Teachers: Here is a chance to have Women's History Month "come alive" in your classroom without extra work on your part.

If it is not convenient for a presenter to visit your classroom on a particular day, please let your principal or school secretary know.

(name and phone number of person coordinating presentations)

ENRICHMENT ACTIVITIES

Collect pictures and articles about women from newspapers, magazines or the Internet. Use them to create women's history posters, collages or bulletin board displays for a classroom, school library, public library or elsewhere.

Create a display using the illustrations in *Profiles of Women Past & Present.*

Assign a biography about a woman for a school book report or read aloud a biography of a woman during Women's History Month in March or anytime during the year.

Research and write a living history monologue, either about a woman in history, or your mother, grandmother or other significant woman in your life.

Write and perform a readers' theater featuring notable women of the past or present.

Write a "Letter to the Editor" emphasizing the importance of celebrating women's history.

Watch a television clip, movie, video, DVD, CD-ROM, or visit the women's history websites included in the Suggested Resources list to learn more about the contributions of women to history.

Create a crossword puzzle or word search using names, descriptions or contributions of women in history as clues.

Research and write brief "news" articles about a woman in history answering the Who, What, When, Where, Why and How questions. Use the articles to create a women's history display or newspaper, or a "Women in the News" radio or television interview talk show.

Review a newspaper, history textbook or encyclopedia and tally the number of stories about men and the number of stories about women.

Nominate an outstanding American woman to be considered for induction to the National Women's Hall of Fame. Nominations can be submitted online at: <http://www.greatwomen.org/nominate.php> or mailed to: The National Women's Hall of Fame, 76 Fall Street, Post Office Box 335, Seneca Falls, New York 13148.

Nominate a woman to be honored on a future U.S. commemorative postage stamp. Include the woman's full name, birth and death dates and a thoughtful argument stating her importance in American history. Send to: Citizens' Stamp Advisory Committee, c/o Stamp Development, U.S. Postal Service, 475 L'Enfant Plaza SW, Room 5670, Washington, D.C. 20260–2437.

Use the monologues and costume and prop suggestions in *Profiles of Women Past and Present* to create a "Living Wax Museum."

Research a notable woman of the past or present who shares your birthday and present her mini-biography on your birthday.

Write a thank you note (addressed to a favorite woman who was portrayed) and send it to the woman or girl who portrayed her.

SUGGESTED RESOURCES

Ashby, Ruth and Deborah Gore Ohrn. *Herstory: Women Who Changed the World.* New York: Viking, 1995.

Baldwin, Louis. *Women of Strength: Biographies of 106 Who Have Excelled in Traditionally Male Fields A.D. 61 to the Present.* Jefferson, NC: McFarland & Company, Inc., 1996.

Bataille, Gretchen M. and Laurie Lisa, eds. *Native American Women. A Biographical Dictionary.* 2nd ed. New York: Routledge, 2001.

Cullen-DuPont, Kathryn. *The Encyclopedia of Women's History in America.* New York: Facts on File, Inc., 1996.

Golden, Kristen and Barbara Findlen. *Remarkable Women of the Twentieth Century: 100 Portraits of Achievement.* New York: Michael Friedman Publishing Group, Inc., 1998.

Hine, Darlene Clark, ed. *Black Women in America. An Historical Encyclopedia.* Brooklyn, NY: Carlson Publishing, Inc., 1993.

Hine, Darlene Clark, ed. *Facts on File Encyclopedia of Black Women in America.* New York: Facts on File, Inc., 1997.

Howard, Angela M. and Frances M. Kavenick. *Handbook of American Women's History.* 2nd ed. Thousand Oaks, CA: Sage Publications, 2000.

James, Edward T., ed. *Notable American Women 1607–1950: A Biographical Dictionary.* Cambridge, MA: Belknap Press of Harvard University Press, 1974.

Kass-Simon, G. and Patricia Farnes, eds. *Women of Science: Righting the Record.* Bloomington, IN: Indiana University Press, 1990.

Palmisano, Joseph M., ed. *Notable Hispanic Women.* Book II. Detroit: Gale Research, Inc., 1998.

Saari, Peggy, ed. *Prominent Women of the 20th Century.* New York: U.X.L., 1996.

Schenken, Suzanne O'Dea. *From Suffrage to the Senate: An Encyclopedia of American Women in Politics.* Santa Barbara, CA: ABC-CLIO, 1999.

Sherrow, Victoria. *A to Z of American Women Business Leaders and Entrepreneurs.* New York: Facts on File, Inc., 2002.

Sicherman, Barbara and Carol Hurd Green, eds. *Notable American Women: The Modern Period.* Cambridge, MA: Belknap Press of Harvard University Press, 1980.

Smith, Jessie Carney, ed. *Notable Black American Women.* Detroit: Gale Research, Inc., 1991.

Sonneborn, Liz. *A to Z of Native American Women.* New York: Facts on File, Inc., 1998.

Telgen, Diane and Jim Kamp, eds. *Notable Hispanic American Women.* Detroit: Gale Research, Inc., 1993.

Woolum, Janet. *Outstanding American Women Athletes: Who They Are and How They Influenced Sports in America.* Phoenix, AZ: Oryx Press, 1992.

Zierdt-Warshaw, Linda, Alan Winkler and Leonard Bernstein. *American Women in Technology: An Encyclopedia.* Santa Barbara, CA: ABC-CLIO, 2000.

Websites

National Women's Hall of Fame. <http://www.greatwomen.org>.

National Women's History Museum. <http://www.nmwh.org>.

National Women's History Project. <http://www.nwhp.org/>.

Women's History. About, Inc. <http://www.womenshistory.about.com>.

AMERICAN
ASSOCIATION OF
UNIVERSITY
WOMEN

AAUW Information

The American Association of University Women (AAUW), founded in 1881, is the oldest and largest national organization promoting equity for all women and girls, lifelong learning and positive societal change. In principle and in practice, AAUW values and seeks a diverse membership. There shall be no barriers to full participation in this organization on the basis of gender, race, creed, age, sexual orientation, national origin or disability.

Membership in AAUW is open to all graduates holding a bachelor's or higher degree from a regionally-accredited college or university. Student affiliate membership is open to anyone enrolled in an associate's or bachelor's program at an accredited two- or four-year college or university. For information about joining AAUW, call 1-800-821-4364 or visit the organization's website: <http://www.aauw.org/>.

A portion of the proceeds from sales of *Profiles of Women Past & Present* will be used to fund scholarships and fellowships through the AAUW Educational Foundation. The AAUW Educational Foundation is the largest source of funding in the world exclusively for graduate women. Eligibility criteria and applications for AAUW Educational Foundation fellowships and grants may be downloaded from the organization's website: <http://www.aauw.org/>.

ORDER FORM

PROFILES OF WOMEN PAST & PRESENT

Make check payable to AAUW/Profiles and mail with a copy of this form to:
AAUW Profiles, P.O. Box 4223
Thousand Oaks, CA 91359–1223

VOLUME ORDER DISCOUNTS AVAILABLE: 20% to 40% depending on the number of books ordered. For details, write to the address above or visit our website: <http://www.aauwto.org/>.

Thank you for your order!

	Quantity	Cost (Quantity x $14.95)
Volume 1		
Volume 2		
Volume 3		
Subtotal		
CA residents add sales tax		
Handling		$2.00
Shipping (total quantity x 50¢)		
TOTAL ENCLOSED:		

Name_____

Address _____

City/State/Zip_____

Organization/School _____Phone_____